Gloria Vanderbilt

DESIGNS FOR YOUR HOME

by Phyllis Hingston Roderick

SIMON AND SCHUSTER/THE McCALL PATTERN COMPANY • NEW YORK

Published by Simon and Schuster
A Gulf & Western Corporation
Simon & Schuster Building
1230 Avenue of the Americas
Rockefeller Center
New York, New York 10020
and
The McCall Pattern Company
230 Park Avenue
New York, New York 10017

Designed by Beri Greenwald
Manufactured in the United States of America
by Rand McNally & Company
1 2 3 4 5 6 7 8 9 10

Library of Congress Cataloging in Publication Data

Vanderbilt, Gloria, date.
  Gloria Vanderbilt designs for your home.

  1. Textile crafts. 2. Handicraft. 3. Interior decoration—Amateurs' manuals. I. Roderick, Phyllis Hingston. II. Title. III. Title: Designs for your home.
  TT699.V36   745.5   77-2281

ISBN 0-671-22637-1

CONTENTS

The Quality of Life, 7

Who Is Gloria? 9

This is Gloria's Art, 10

CHAPTER ONE COLLAGE, 13

CHAPTER TWO DECOUPAGE, 27

CHAPTER THREE NEEDLEPOINT, 47

CHAPTER FOUR AFGHANS, 83

CHAPTER FIVE TABLE ART, 93

CHAPTER SIX SOME OF GLORIA'S FAVORITE THINGS, 107

CHAPTER SEVEN BASKETS ARE AN ART FORM, TOO, 131

CHAPTER EIGHT TREASURES FROM THE SEA, 141

CHAPTER NINE THE HOLIDAY SEASON, 157

CHAPTER TEN SOME OF GLORIA'S FAVORITE GIFTS, 181

CHAPTER ELEVEN GLORIA IN MINIATURE, 197

Shopping Information, 223

Contributing Designers, 224

THE
QUALITY
OF
LIFE

By

Gloria Vanderbilt

There is an impulse in each of us to make, in some manner, a very personal and individual mark on the world around us. The little child, coming upon a stretch of clean white snow, gleefully rushes to imprint the shapes of his feet upon it. A woman, passing through a strange room, pauses briefly to move an object on a table, making a slight rearrangement that may go unnoticed by others, but to her eye is more pleasing. A boy carves his initials upon a tree. A girl places a daisy secretly against the grass. We all write our names upon the sand.

All of us hope that our choices, our actions, our influences will make a little sweeter, for our having been there, those rooms we enter, those worlds we move through, those lives we touch, those people and those places we leave behind us.

The effort to do so is, in a way, our small gesture toward immortality, our little message to the universe. It says, "I was here" to the ages.

The first lady who planted flowers around the entrance to her cave, or rearranged the rocks her family sat upon, or made a bedspread of tiger skins, was only doing what we try to do today: to make our surroundings reflect our better feelings about ourselves; to create an ambiance that expresses our enthusiasm about life and beauty and grace and harmony. The same impulse led us to invent song and dance and pictures, and is inherent in that part of us that dreams and invents . . . that is reckless and restless and fanciful.

Each of us in some way participates in the spirit of the artist. We share his hunger and his passion and something of his vision. (Which is also her hunger and her passion and her vision, for artistry knows no gender.) We share the artist's compulsion to give form and permanence to what is formless, impermanent and eternally elusive; we share the compulsion to define the undefinable, translate the untranslatable, and express the inexpressible. All of us know something of the artist's lust and fire and anger and soul and sensation. It is the artist in us that makes beauty and meaning out of what seems like chaos and confusion; that creates, from bits and pieces and the flotsam and jetsam around us, something new that has balance and order and coherence.

People sometimes ask me if my children show signs of artistic talent. I answer that all children are talented. Every child is unique and individual and has his own way of seeing. The child's world is one of expectation and discovery and wonder. What he is goes into his paintings, into his play. It is precisely that child's freedom of inquiry, that sense of expectation, that willingness to respond, that eagerness to express, that we should cherish and encourage and nourish, both in our children and in ourselves, for it is somewhere in that region of our minds and imaginations and fantasies that our most valuable selves reside. Somewhere there is a divine, godlike and creative part of ourselves that we too often lose touch with.

Too often, as a part of the price we pay in growing up, we lose or we have smothered out of us, or frightened out of us, that blessed innocence, that sense of wonder, that trust; we stop looking and seeing and feeling with the clear, clean eyes of youth; we stop growing and start mistrusting ourselves, our impulses, our tastes, our instincts, our judgments. We let other people tell us what we think, what we like, what we feel. For those who look, who see, who respond—for those who are not afraid to trust their creative impulses or to expose something of what is inside them . . . those who recognize their own need for expression, whether it is in painting a picture, hanging wallpaper, making a dress, baking a roast, or taking a walk and looking—really looking—at the trees, the grass, the flowers, the houses, the sky, the faces they pass—for those who can do this and really experience it, without fear of others' judgments or apprehension about others' opinions, life can never be leaden or boring or aimless. Life is a transient and fleeting thing and we change every day. Look well at your child's face today. Tomorrow it will already be different. This is the only day in all his life that he will look exactly like that.

Wherever I go, no matter to whom I'm invited to speak, what I have to say is always the same. "Don't be afraid." Don't be afraid to leave yourself open to experience, to looking and seeing and responding. Life is a long process of seeking. We seek meaning in the world around us and we seek the truth of ourselves.

Just as every child has genius—he has to have, if you consider the astonishing sum of skills he has to master, the incredible amount of information he has to learn, the endless lessons in living he must absorb—just as he has genius, so have you. Each of you has locked in your heart and mind a world of experience unique unto yourself; insights known only by you, thoughts and memories and wishes and hopes and dreams that are yours alone. Whatever your opinion of yourself—whatever you think of your accomplishments, your successes or your failures—you can say to yourself, "I am me." I am unique and unprecedented. There is only one of me in all eternity. I have a creative soul and I must trust it. I must encourage it, prod it, provoke it. I have my own will, my own courage, my own strength, my own perception and my own vision. I say, "Don't be afraid." I say be free. Know that you are free. Let each day be a new beginning. Each day is a space of time in which there are things to be found, things to learn, things to do. Don't be afraid to look at things anew. See those things you might have missed before. Don't be afraid to leave the door open, or to open it. Life holds joy and it holds pain, and each of us experiences both. Both are part of living. Both are teachers and we must learn from both. We must love the joy in us and love the pain in us, for without either there is no life. Cherish them. Use them.

Open doors. We are never too old to start and never old enough to stop. We must leave the door open to new beginnings, new experiences, new insights, new ideas, new dreams.

Life is precious. My life is precious. Your life is precious. The lives of those others who share our lives are precious. We must dare to do. We must give of that better part of ourselves. We must draw upon that well of creativity inside us, and when we reach out to make our mark on the world around us, it will truly be our mark—something we felt, something we found, something we made. We can enrich our own living and give richness to the living of those whose lives we touch. This earth is ours for a time. Be part of it. So, be yourself. Move to your own music. Listen to your own heart. Cherish your passion, your pain, your laughter, your joy. Treasure all love.

Seek truth. Love beauty. Embrace life.

WHO IS GLORIA?

THIS IS GLORIA. Artist, designer and author, Gloria Vanderbilt has also been, at different times, an actress, a poet and a literary critic. She has been called a "feminine version of Renaissance man" with good reason. But first and always she is an artist, and that handsome tribute seems somehow a little heavy-handed for a creature of delicate sensibility whose essential talent is a unique responsiveness to people and to every form of beauty. She lives in a sparkling world of color and pattern created by her own artwork and the exuberant fabrics she has designed. Bed and bath fashions, table linens and dinnerware also bear her joyous imprint. Now her art and design have been translated into fascinating needlework and craft projects creative people can reproduce. Some of the sparkling ideas are so simple, no detailed directions are necessary, but most are complete with step-by-step directions and diagrams that are very easy to follow. Miss Vanderbilt once said, "Art is a dream. It only comes true when you reach people with it. Then the dream becomes real." With this book, her dream of brighter, happier living surrounded by beauty and color becomes real and very possible for many people.

Gloria Vanderbilt is also Mrs. Wyatt Cooper. Below left, her husband, a well-known writer. Below, Mrs. Cooper with her two young sons, Carter and Anderson.

THIS
IS
GLORIA'S
ART

Gloria Vanderbilt has been painting since she was ten years old, and, during the last decade, has revitalized the art of collage to such a degree that "re-created" might be a more accurate term to describe the impact of her work on this art form. Her paintings and collages have been exhibited by major galleries and museums, and are owned by many private collectors. An innovator as well as an artist, she has pioneered in unexplored media and invented new techniques. Each brilliant, highly personal work is an explosion of color and pattern that expresses—and communicates—her intense joy in pure creation.

"Still Life with Tiger Lilies" is anything but still. Placed on a table that pulsates with pattern, the vivid bouquet seems to be swept with motion. Signed lithograph is 28" x 22".

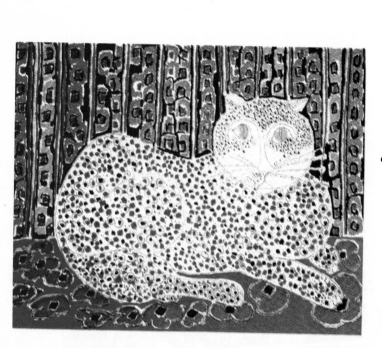

Feline "Felicie's Oyster" looks at life with unblinking eyes, unperturbed and enigmatic. Unframed lithograph, left, is 22" x 28".

"**E**lizabeth the Queen" is perhaps the most renowned of Miss Vanderbilt's many elaborate collages. Shimmering with aluminum foil and silver lace, the imposing 59" x 40" composition occupies a place of honor in the artist's own household.

COLLAGE

COLLAGE: THE ACCESSIBLE ART

Collage is an art form, but don't let that definition deter you from the fun of engaging in this easy, inexpensive, freewheeling form of self-expression. No other kind of artistic endeavor encourages you to be so completely yourself. And collage is an art that's accessible to everyone. The materials—and the inspiration—are everywhere about you. Anything that can be pasted to a surface can be used. There are no rules. Surely such freedom in the name of art is good for the soul.

The name of this game may not be totally familiar, but know it or not, you almost certainly have already practiced collage. If, as a child, you ever cut out the shape of a house, or a tree, or a flower, and pasted it on a piece of paper, you created a collage. And if, a little later, you cut out a lopsided red heart and pasted it on a lacy paper doily and pasted *that* on a piece of cardboard to make a Valentine, you were progressing in the creative process called collage. "Collage" comes from the French *coller,* which means to paste or glue. The definition is certainly specific. But the definition is the *only* thing that's specific about collage. *What* is glued or pasted? Practically anything. Any material or object that's lightweight enough to be pasted or fastened to a surface is fair game. Paper and fabric pop into mind because they're so obviously pastable. Paper alone presents endless possibilities. Gloria Vanderbilt, who revolutionized the whole concept of collage, created the dramatic composition at the left with nothing but a variety of papers and paint. There's a list of what she used, plus a diagram, on page 19, if you'd like to duplicate it.

The long and diverse list of paper materials that can be used for collage includes all kinds of craft papers, wrapping papers, wallpapers, foils; magazine ads, newspapers, travel folders, seed catalogs, cigarette packages, comic strips, corrugated containers; postage stamps, ticket stubs, computer cards, adding-machine tape, even confetti. And fabrics aren't far behind when it comes to variety. The many different textures obtainable in fabrics can add fascinating dimension to a collage. Everything from cobwebby lace to crunchy tweed is a possibility. And what a fairyland of colors and textures and tinsel and gilt a good notions counter provides in its ribbons and braids and imaginative trimmings.

All of these things and numerous others that are ideal for working in collage can be found in abun-

"**F**lowers with Wallpaper" collage. Complete directions appear on page 18.

dance in homes and offices and in the streets. Just look around you. Look in your sewing basket, in the drawers of your desk, in that closet where you stash all the odds and ends you've been saving for something, *some* day. The day you decide to try your hand at collage is the day. Anything you've saved because it appealed to you in some way is a good prospect for the nucleus of your first collage. "Use at least one object that you really love in each picture," advises Gloria Vanderbilt. Old photographs of family and friends, greeting cards that have a special meaning, postcards and airplane tickets and other mementos from your travels and vacations will add to the pleasure of selecting and combining and arranging the elements of a collage, and will make it much more meaningful than just an experiment in color and design. Miss Vanderbilt keeps a collection of just such memorabilia in her studio, in addition to the bits and pieces of paper and fabric she uses so effectively in her work. She keeps her materials, tools and equipment all together in an old drafting table with lots of narrow drawers—the best kind of filing cabinet for such a varied assortment. "It helps to be organized," she says. She doesn't try to decide in advance how to use all the bits and pieces she's constantly accumulating. "As long as they please you," she comments, "they'll eventually find their way into a composition." Once you begin thinking in terms of collage, you, too, will become an avid collector of all manner of objects, because you'll be seeing things with new eyes and noticing things you never noticed before.

All the objects and elements employed in a collage can be "found" materials, and the only necessary tools are just as easy to come by. Scissors or a razor blade and paste are the only essentials, but you may want to include waterproof ink markers and crayons for adding touches of color and India ink for drawing lines or adding detail. Miss Vanderbilt also uses tweezers and a mat knife, and keeps an iron on hand for pressing fabrics. She prefers gesso board for backing because she likes its smooth texture and the whiteness of its surface. But any art board or even cardboard will do nicely for a start if it's stiff enough not to buckle when paste is applied or objects are glued to it. Masonite, plywood, woodboard and canvas board are also used if a substantial backing is desirable. If you want a white surface (a good idea when applying

fabrics) without bothering to buy gesso board, you can apply a thin coat of white paint to whatever board you're using. Acrylic paint is best because it won't turn yellow, but any white paint is satisfactory. Miss Vanderbilt uses spray-on glue because it's easy to control, but a strong white glue applied with a brush is the usual choice.

Everyone who works in collage develops his own methods of achieving the effects he wants. We'd like to tell you a little about the way Miss Vanderbilt works because the results are so stunningly successful, and because you'll see many examples of her work in this book. Like other major collagists, she tends to let the materials she's working with take the lead, and is a great believer in allowing one's subconscious to guide the creative process. "Try not to think," she advises. "Trust your impulse. Let your instinct and your natural creative impulse take over." That's all very well for an artist, you're probably thinking, but I wouldn't even know how to begin. Well, try it. If you've assembled some suitable materials that appeal to you, and you're really fond of even a few of them, start with one or two of your favorites and place them on the board you're using. You'll see an immediate relation between the shapes and textures of the objects or materials and the board itself. That relationship will be either pleasing or displeasing. If it's displeasing, you'll instinctively reach out to move the objects around. If you like it, you'll find yourself glancing at the rest of your materials to see what other textures and shapes and colors would add to it. Before you know it, you'll have a pleasing arrangement that is attractive in itself and also has meaning and importance to you because you started with something you really like. Collage is just as simple as that. The first collage Miss Vanderbilt created happened by accident because a paper lace mat she'd been attracted to was lying around her studio. She was going through a stack of magazines when she came across it. Just for fun, she cut it to fit the shapes of a headpiece and collar on the portrait of an Alsatian girl she was starting to work on. *Voilà!* The effect was fascinating, and that painting immediately became a collage.

Whatever the inspiration for a new collage, and whatever other elements it suggests, Miss Vanderbilt arranges and rearranges the elements many times before deciding on the final composition. Even when satisfied with a particular arrangement,

"Lady in Gingham" is Miss Vanderbilt's first collage portrait of Queen Elizabeth. Once she began doing elaborately ornamental figures in this medium, she became fascinated with the fantastic court costumes of the Elizabethan period, so richly embellished with lace, embroidery, passementerie, gold and jewels. Interpreting such luxury in plebeian gingham amused her, and is typical of the whimsy in much of her work.

The figure was sketched directly on gesso board measuring a sizable 60" x 40". Pieces of clay paper back the fabrics, which are encrusted with white and silver lace and silvery flowers. The crown is aluminum foil, the jewels glittery gift paper. Paper lace is mounted on gingham for the butterflies, on foil for the flowers. A later and even more elaborate portrait of Queen Elizabeth appears on page 11.

she allows herself enough time to look at it again before beginning to paste the elements down. She believes a picture is never really finished. "It simply stops at a good place," she says, "and long after that, you may suddenly have the feeling that something is missing and that a few more touches of color or detail would improve it." She notes that this has happened to her, and that she didn't hesitate to do so.

Miss Vanderbilt is both a perfectionist and an innovator, and a constant search for fresh, new variations on familiar themes is a characteristic of her work. To her the opportunity for exploration and experimentation that collage affords is one of its greatest charms. "One of the reasons collage is never boring," she says, "is the constant surprise of discovering a new way of doing something you've done before." Her "Lady in Gingham," opposite, is just one variation on one of her favorite themes.

Getting down to some of the specific techniques that make Miss Vanderbilt's work in collage so expressive, you've probably noticed that the way she handles fabrics and papers seems to give them visual mobility. A flat piece of fabric loses its static quality and seems capable of motion. The effect is no accident. She often shreds the edges of fabrics she uses to give them life and vitality. To do this, she uses one blade of her scissors as a cutting edge, pulling the fabric along it in the general shape she wants to obtain. This is especially effec- tive when layering one fabric over another, and keeps the lower fabric from looking flattened and lifeless. As you've probably also noticed, she uses lots of lace in her collages, which also seems to have a life of its own. This is because she seldom cuts the delicate fabric with a hard, straight line. Instead, she carefully separates the motif or section she's removing by snipping each little connecting thread. The tiny ends of threads still attached to the flower—let's say—seem to quiver with life, lending the flower or motif a dynamic quality.

Miss Vanderbilt works mainly with papers and fabrics pasted on gesso board, and also combines this form of collage with painting in India ink or crayon. Whichever technique she uses, her style is so distinctive that her work is immediately recognizable to anyone who has been exposed to it. But collage really is an "accessible art," and there are many other forms of it. Some fabric collage is done solely with fabrics, even to the backing material, with the additional layers or cutouts sewn to the background. Canvas, sailcloth, felt and even interfacing material have been used for this purpose.

Many other materials can be used for collage; there are creative possibilities in almost anything you can think of. Whole compositions have been done entirely in string, for instance, and the texture and dimension that can be achieved with even this mundane material are amazing. Large seeds, dried grasses and flowers, seashells and feathers have all been utilized in collage, and some artists work in nothing but wood, with bark and driftwood the popular choices in this category. A surprisingly representative picture can be made with nothing but buttons, or bits of costume jewelry. Another type of collage employs objects made of metal—nuts and bolts, metal tubing, machine parts, even kitchen equipment, cans and other containers. Your imagination is the only limit when it comes to materials.

Whatever materials or objects you decide to use, approach working in collage with a sense of discovery and adventure. Any kind of artistic endeavor is an adventure, and collage is more so than most because there's no way of knowing in advance how it will turn out or what the final result will be. As you arrange and rearrange the different elements, and experiment with new materials, you may learn a great deal about such things as color and design, and balance and harmony—and even more about yourself. You may even discover that you are an artist!

"FLOWERS WITH WALLPAPER" COLLAGE

Gloria Vanderbilt's "Flowers with Wallpaper" collage, shown on page 14, illustrates her typical technique of combining collage with painting. It is approximately 20″ x 20″ and was done on gesso board. Cut board at least 21″ x 21″ to allow for framing, and prime with white acrylic or semigloss paint if not using gesso board.

Numbers on diagram indicate colors and materials used in original. The decorative "wallpaper" background was drawn in on original with India ink and accented with free-form circles in paint and paper cutouts to suggest a fruit motif. Fine lines in diagram indicate detail in this area, which can be transferred to board if you're copying original exactly. Instead of drawing, you could cover this area with real wallpaper in a delicate stripe.

Enlarge diagram onto paper ruled in 2″ squares. If covering background with wallpaper, apply that first. Transfer outline of lace-paper doily, which represents table and is numbered 1 in diagram, and paste doily in place. Following diagram and list of materials, apply other cutouts. Layer flower cutouts concentrically, starting with largest cutout first and building up flowers that represent large, full-blown roses. Allow paste used to apply each cutout to dry before adding the next one. If drawing "wallpaper" background, fill in this area after flower and leaf cutouts have been applied.

Avoid tracing as much as possible to retain free-form effect of original. Small painted leaves and circle cutouts could be done freehand instead of being traced.

You won't be able to duplicate some of the materials used exactly; substitute similar objects or create your own versions. For instance, the "flower-child" cutout is from an old print which was pasted on a circle of lavender paper, mounted on aluminum foil and framed in a lacy gilt paper frame. You could use an old photograph and paste it on a flower cut from paper. Small gilt paper frames similar to the one in the collage are available at craft shops which sell decoupage materials. Use silvery wrapping paper or aluminum foil for the tray and circle it with narrow gold paper braid, available from craft shops, or with any narrow metallic trim.

After cutouts have been pasted in place, outline doily and small leaves with frilly, free-hand detail in pen and ink to increase the lacy effect of the whole thing.

Miss Vanderbilt is especially pleased by the combinations of orange-red, cyclamen red and magenta in flowers. Since colors in photograph may not reproduce accurately, try to choose your colors according to the color key.

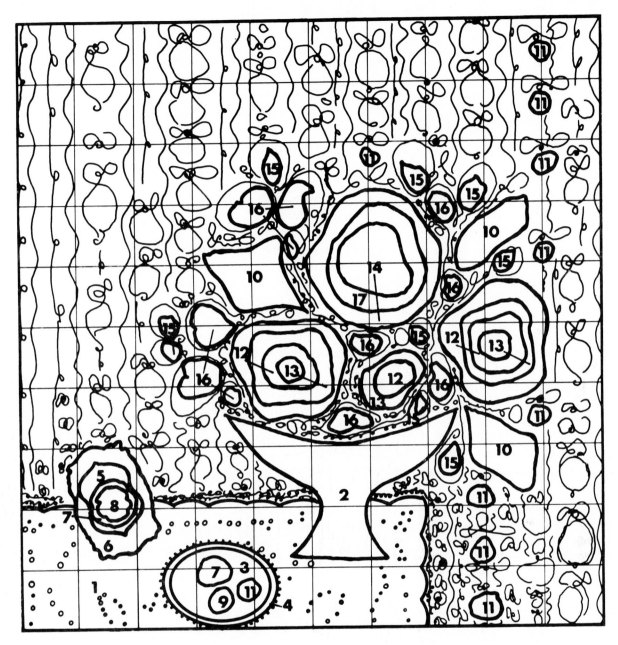

1 square = 2″

Key to Colors and Materials Used in Original Collage

1 White lace-paper doily
2 Purple gift paper
3 Silver mesh paper
4 Gold paper braid
5 Aluminum foil
6 Gilt paper frame
7 Lavender paper
8 "Flower-child"
9 Blue paper
10 Olive green paper
11 Violet paper
12 Cyclamen red paper
13 Orange-red paper
14 Bright pink paper
15 Blue-green leaves
16 Moss green leaves
17 Magenta paper

"PANSIES" COLLAGE

Gloria Vanderbilt's original "Pansies" collage, shown on page 63, is approximately 20″ x 24″, and was done on gesso board. Illustration board or any art board stiff enough not to buckle when paste is applied could be substituted. Board should be at least 21″ x 25″ to allow for framing. Prime board with white acrylic or semigloss paint and allow paint to dry before beginning to paste. Use spray-on glue or white glue and brush applicator for pasting.

Numbers on diagram identify materials Miss Vanderbilt used for background and cutouts; diagram is shown on a graph so you can copy placement exactly, if you wish, by enlarging diagram onto paper ruled in 1″ squares. But since the primary pleasure of working in collage is self-expression, you should feel free to substitute materials of your own choosing and alter or change the arrangement. You may prefer a nosegay of flowers other than pansies, for instance, and you could substitute any gift-wrapping paper you like for the wallpapers used in the original.

The numbers on the diagram that refer to the list of original materials also indicate the order in which the materials were applied to produce the three-dimensional effect of the collage. After diagram has been enlarged, transfer the vertical lines that separate the background areas numbered 1 and 2 onto the primed board. Then, using a ruler, extend both lines to full length of board. Cut pieces of fabric to cover both areas, adding 1½″ beyond edges of board so that each piece can be wrapped around edges of board and glued to the back of it. Place each piece of fabric in position along marked lines and tape in place temporarily on right side of board. Turn board over and apply glue to wrong side of extending fabric and to edges of board. Pull fabric around edges and press firmly to back of board, mitering corners. Remove tape from right side of board.

Draw or trace outline of area numbered 3 on board. Cut fabric to fit, and glue to board in same manner as before. After removing tape, apply a small amount of glue to right side of board (actually to previously applied fabrics) below edges of third fabric. Do not apply glue directly to this piece; just press firmly in place.

Using enlarged diagram, transfer outlines of vase, mat, other free-form cutouts and remaining materials to collage if following original. You won't, of course, be able to duplicate flowers and butterflies exactly, but you can place similar cutouts in approximately the same positions without tracing outlines. Arrange any other substitutions directly on collage and proceed with pasting. Where cutouts are layered, glue in place in numerical order. Allow each cutout to dry before pasting another one over it.

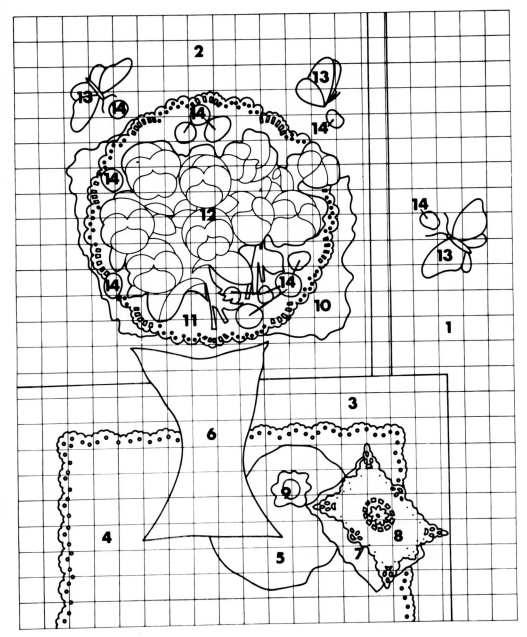

1 square = 1″

Key to Materials Used in Original Collage

1 Violet gingham, 1″ checks
2 Violet linen-textured fabric
3 Rose-printed linen
4 Lacy white paper place mat
5 Beige-background wallpaper
6 Grey-background wallpaper
7 Scrap of yellow linen
8 White lace-paper valentine
9 Flower cutout
10 Violet gingham, ⅛″ checks
11 Border from round paper doily
12 Pansies cut from old prints
13 Butterflies cut from old prints
14 Yellow, green, pink linen and paper cutouts

HANDS ACROSS THE TABLE

"His" and "her" hands, each offering the other a decorative posy—a delightfully symbolic way to say "love" or "peace." Gloria Vanderbilt did the originals, opposite, in crayon, India ink and Magic Marker, for you to copy exactly or translate into your favorite medium. For the collages on this page, we matched the vibrant colors in a variety of fabrics, embroidered the flowers and leaves with French knots and cross-stitching, then added dimension with seed beads, buttons, braid and black cording. Enlarge the charts and go to it!

"HANDS" PAINTINGS

Gloria Vanderbilt's original paintings were done with Caran D'ache neo-crayons, Magic Marker and India ink on clay-coated paper. Wax crayons, paint or any medium preferred can be substituted for the neo-crayons; any smooth-surfaced drawing paper can be used. Paintings are approximately 11½" x 13½"; paper should be at least 13½" x 15½" to allow for framing. Miss Vanderbilt used 15¾" x 19½" paper; frames shown in photograph are 16¼" x 20¼".

Paintings can be copied freehand from diagrams, or diagrams can be enlarged on paper ruled in ½" squares, and then transferred to drawing paper by using dressmakers' tracing paper.

Use Magic Marker for outlines indicated by heavy black lines. Apply color where indicated by solid areas in diagrams. Since colors may not be reproduced accurately in photograph, color key describes colors in original paintings. The irregular outlines of solid areas in the diagrams are result of color being applied to originals with freehand strokes; apply color in same manner rather than trying to follow outlines exactly. Use pen and India ink for details indicated by fine lines in diagrams. In original paintings, some details were drawn in before color was applied, but most were drawn in afterward. In either case, small details such as tiny circles in flowers and crosses in leaves should be drawn in freehand to approximate the spontaneity of original paintings. Spray finished paintings with acrylic sealer.

All the detail in the original paintings is included in the diagrams; we simplified some of it when embroidering the collages. Feel free to substitute your own selection of fabrics and trimmings and add more or less detail as desired.

"HANDS" COLLAGES

Collages interpret Miss Vanderbilt's paintings in fabric and trimmings. Backgrounds are unbleached muslin; you'll need a piece at least 13½" x 15½" for each collage. We used a variety of cotton fabrics (mostly polished cotton and sailcloth) for the solid-color areas, matching colors in paintings as closely as possible. (Color key describes colors in original paintings.) ¼ yard each of the first nine colors listed and ½ yard of violet for the borders is enough for both collages. Where possible, we shredded the edges of the cutout fabrics to approximate the irregular outlines of the paintings.

Use paper ruled in ½" squares to enlarge diagrams, omitting detail indicated by fine lines. Cen-ter enlarged diagram on muslin and transfer heavy outlines of flowers, leaves and hands (including cuffs and sleeves) onto muslin, using dressmakers' tracing paper. Also transfer outline of border. Stretch muslin taut on a piece of cardboard and hold in place with thumbtacks around the edges.

From enlarged diagrams, cut out sections indicated by solid areas in original diagrams to use as patterns for fabric cutouts. Trace each pattern on fabric and cut out. Spread white glue sparingly on the back of each cutout and press firmly on muslin, using transferred outlines as guidelines.

Using black Magic Marker, go over outlines of flowers, stems and leaves. Draw small, scallopy "flowers" on borders with black Magic Marker. On both collages, tack black cording over outlines of hands. Remove muslin from cardboard and em-

COLOR KEY

1 Chinese red
2 Hot pink
3 Apple green
4 Pale olive green
5 Periwinkle blue
6 Teal blue
7 Dark blue-purple
8 Cinnamon brown
9 Rich red-violet
10 Violet
11 Lemon yellow
12 Yellow-orange

broider small cross-stitches on leaves with black embroidery floss. We used a square black button for center of each flower and tacked black seed beads around inner circle. Large zigzag circles on "her" flower and small circles on both flowers were worked with black embroidery floss. To make small circle, begin French knot but do not pull thread tight; hold knot open by tacking floss in place opposite original stitch.

Up to this point, fabrics, trimmings and embroidery have been applied to both collages in the same manner, but treatment of the sleeves and cuffs differs.

We outlined "his" sleeve and cuff with black soutache braid, drew black lines on the sleeve with black Magic Marker, added white tucked fabric for the cuff and sewed on a wine-colored button for the cuff link.

We used two-tone embroidered braid for "her" cuff and embroidered squiggly black lines between the two colors. We outlined the top of "her" sleeve with soutache braid, then switched to black looped braid to outline the cuff. We embroidered the wavy black lines on the sleeve and sewed black seed beads in straight rows between them.

DECOUPAGE

DECOUPAGE: A CUTUP'S PRIMER

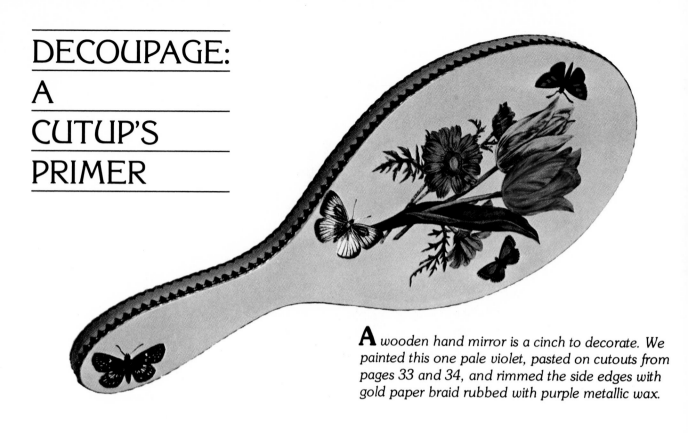

A wooden hand mirror is a cinch to decorate. We painted this one pale violet, pasted on cutouts from pages 33 and 34, and rimmed the side edges with gold paper braid rubbed with purple metallic wax.

Decoupage, a form of collage, is the art of decorating surfaces with applied paper cutouts. The word comes from the French *découper,* meaning to cut up or cut out. Although a more definite and limited art form than collage, like collage, anyone can do it.

Decoupage can be used to decorate things made of many different materials—wood, metal, glass, plastic, ceramics, even leather. On pages 35–37, you'll see some ideas for decorating several different kinds of surfaces. But for a first project, it is best to select something made of raw wood. Craft shops sell a wide variety of wooden objects that are easy to work on, and will be useful as well as decorative when they are finished. Try to select something with fairly large, flat surfaces for your first project. And check to make sure that the edges are smooth and any corners (on boxes, for instance) are neatly glued. If you plan to stain the piece instead of painting it first, notice the appearance of the grain, and whether or not there are any obvious flaws which will show through the stain. Maple, walnut, white pine and poplar are all easy to work on; open-grained woods such as mahogany are not.

The next step is deciding how to decorate the piece.

Pictures and motifs for use in decoupage can be cut from any smooth, medium-weight paper. Fairly lightweight paper is best for the intricate cutting enjoyed by experienced practitioners, but very thin papers become too fragile to handle when moist with paste, and thick, pulpy papers cannot be cut in delicate patterns and are difficult to cover with varnish. Craft shops carry a wide selection of prints made especially for decoupage; originals or reproductions of hand-colored eighteenth-century prints are the most interesting and the most authentic-looking for use in this craft which dates back two hundred years and was wildly popular during the Victorian era. Some fine old prints from Gloria Vanderbilt's collection are reproduced on pages 33 and 34. They'll do very nicely for your first projects, and were used to decorate the boxes and mirror shown here and on the following page. Of course, it's preferable to use prints without printing on the back, so the cutouts are repeated at the back of this book. If you want to use a cutout from a magazine, a thin coat of white paint brushed over the back of the page will obscure any printing. (Using a medium to dark background color for the cutouts also helps.) Cutouts used to decorate any object should have a common theme; pick a subject that interests you and use related motifs. Of course, any elements cut from a single print will be compatible. Choose prints that don't require too much intricate cutting at first.

After you've decided what cutouts to use, choose a background color that will show them off to advantage. Matching a color used in a small area of the print is almost always effective. Deciding whether to use paint, stain or an antiquing glaze on the background comes next.

Paint supplies a smooth, solid color which shows off fine cutting and the colors in the prints. Antiqued backgrounds are painted and then glazed with another color. Stains are usually natural wood tones, but there are also metallic waxes in brighter colors which act as stains. Whatever finish you decide on, sand all surfaces before applying the back-

ground color. Use garnet paper or any finishing grade of sandpaper wrapped around a small sanding block. Sand in the direction of the grain until all surfaces are smooth to the touch, but be careful not to sand corners round. At this point, any hardware to be attached with screws should be installed so that any necessary holes or notches are made in the raw wood.

Many of the wood boxes carried by craft shops can be used as handbags if latches and handles are applied. The box with the two interchangeable panels was designed to be used as a handbag that could complement several different costumes, but we liked it so well as a box, we left it that way. Most boxes and all handbags require hinges. For recessed hinges, cut the necessary notches into the back of the box and the lid and install the hinges. Then remove them and any other hardware and label for use later. Doing so at this point prevents any possibility of ruining your project by having to drill holes or cut into the finished piece. Paint and

This box comes with two separate panels which fit into slots behind the cutout front for a shadow-box effect. We covered the box with dollhouse wallpaper, decorated one panel with cutouts from page 33.

A small house-shaped box is a haven for birds—the paper variety, cut from page 34. The roof was first covered with dollhouse roof paper. For shopping information on boxes, mirror and papers, see page 223.

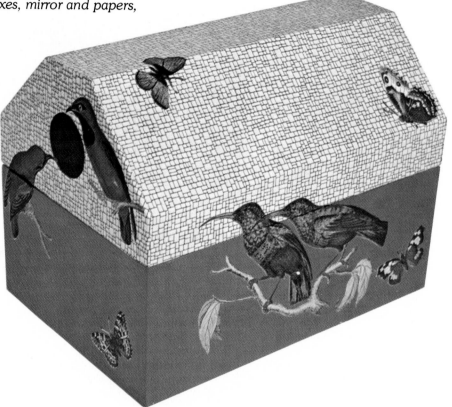

other finishes will get into the screw holes while you're working, but this will only make for a tighter fit.

PAINT, STAIN OR GLAZE

A good brush is required to produce a professional-looking painted background. Choose a soft oxhair brush, if possible, about ½″ wide and clean in warm, sudsy water after each use. Apply a coat of acrylic sealer first, allow it to dry and sand lightly with a finishing grade of sandpaper. Always clean the surface with a tack cloth after sanding and before applying either paint or finish. For a very smooth, hard surface, or if wood is open-grained, apply two coats of gesso, one with the grain, the second against it, allowing each to dry thoroughly. When dry, dry-sand the gesso with #320 wet-or-dry sandpaper. Stir the paint to mix thoroughly and dip brush only halfway into the paint. Brush paint on in the direction of the grain, thinly and

evenly. Start all strokes on unpainted wood and brush into already painted area. Apply three coats, sanding between the second and third coats, with wet-or-dry sandpaper used dry. Allow paint to dry and seal with three coats of acrylic spray before beginning to paste cutouts in place.

To antique a painted surface, brush or wipe on antiquing glaze, completely covering the paint. Wait a few minutes and wipe off with a pad made of cheesecloth or other soft fabric. Wipe from one side of the piece and then from the other to remove glaze evenly. Wait twenty-four hours before proceeding if you plan to use varnish as a finishing coat. If lacquer is to be used, apply three or four coats of clear acrylic spray, which will make the glaze dry faster.

To stain raw wood, shake stain to mix thoroughly and wipe into wood with a sponge, in direction of grain. Wipe off excess with a cloth or paper towel. Allow stain to dry and polish with #0000 steel wool. Wipe clean with tack cloth and spray with three light coats of acrylic sealer. When dry, sand lightly with wet-or-dry sandpaper used dry.

PREPARING YOUR PRINT

There are so many beautifully colored prints available, and so many attractive illustrations to be found, you'll probably have a hard time deciding which ones to use. Even so, you don't have to use either one exactly as you find them. Colors of small areas can be brightened by using colored oil pencils, or even changed by gently erasing and then recoloring. Fine lines or tiny areas that are too delicate to cut out can be thickened or enlarged by using the oil pencils. And if certain areas of the print, such as flower stems, seem so delicate or divorced from larger areas that they might break off, you can draw connecting lines or "ladders" to help keep them intact, cutting away the "ladders" just before pasting. Touch-ups completed, the print must be sealed before cutting to make the paper less likely to tear and to keep the colors from bleeding. Sealing also helps the finish adhere to the print. Spray on two thin coats of clear acrylic sealer, making sure the edges of the print are well covered.

CUTTING AND ARRANGING

The care with which you cut out the designs you have chosen will make a great difference in the appearance of your finished piece. Use sharp, curved scissors with slender points, such as cuticle scissors. They should fit your hand well and feel comfortable in use. Hold the scissors with your thumb and third finger, with the blades resting on your index finger and the points turned away from the paper. Held in this position, with your palm facing upward, the tilted scissors will bevel the edge of the paper as you cut.

Holding the print with your other hand, feed it carefully into the scissors, moving the print back and forth while keeping the scissors motionless. Hold the print lightly so it's easy to move around. The important thing is not to cut a straight or hard edge. The edge should be minutely serrated to look natural and blend into the background. Wiggle the print back and forth as you feed it into the scissors to achieve this effect. Start cutting at the center of the print and work outward. When fin-

ished cutting, color with the oil pencils any white edges that show.

Now comes the part you'll probably enjoy most: arranging the different parts of the design. You'll rarely want to use all the parts of a print in their original positions. It's much more fun to make up your own design to fit your particular project. Cut the motifs apart and rearrange as you like, trimming them to fit if necessary. You can draw a flat diagram of the object you're decorating on a large piece of paper and do your arranging on that, if you like. You may find it more fun to do it right on the box or whatever—holding the cutouts temporarily in place with a dab of removable adhesive, which is sold in craft shops.

PASTING THINGS DOWN

Doing a good job when it comes to pasting your cutouts in place is obviously important. If not pasted down securely, they'll come loose in spots later, no matter how many coats of finish are applied over them. If you're working on a box or a handbag, hold the lid in place temporarily with dabs of removable adhesive at the corners. If your cutouts are of thin, lightweight paper, or are delicate and lacy, use special decoupage paste, which does not dry quickly; you'll be able to move the cutouts around a bit if you're not completely satisfied with the placement as planned. Use a liquid white glue if pasting down heavy paper or if the background is highly polished or varnished. This type of glue is harder to work with because it dries almost immediately. Using a half-and-half mixture of decoupage paste and white glue works well with most papers and gives you the advantages of both. You can apply the adhesive either to the cutouts or to the wood surface, using your finger or a small brush. The important thing is to have a thin, even coat between the two. If applying adhesive to a cutout, be sure the entire back surface is evenly covered. Do not overlap the edges of cutouts; cut them so they fit together with edges just meeting.

Place your cutout in position and gently pat it down with a slightly dampened cloth or soft sponge. Then place a slightly damp cloth over the cutout and use a brayer—a small rubber roller designed for this purpose—to smooth the print in place while rolling out excess glue, from the center outward. The slightly damp cloth will pick up the excess glue. Excess glue can also be removed by pressing the fleshy part of your forefinger down on the print in a rolling motion, moving outward from the center. Wipe excess glue away immediately with a barely damp sponge. When glue is dry, gently press down the edges of the cutout with the curved end of a burnisher. A burnisher is a small metal tool with one pointed end and one paddle-shaped end. This will bevel the edges of the print and press them into the wood. If any edge of the cutout doesn't stay pasted down, apply more glue with one end of a toothpick. Reburnish the edge and make sure all excess glue is removed. Glue any additional elements such as borders or paper braid in place and burnish in the same manner. Allow either paste or glue to dry thoroughly, preferably overnight.

If your design calls for a cutout to be placed over the dividing line between a box and its lid, paste it in position in one piece and allow glue to dry thoroughly. Then cut through the print where the edges of the box and lid meet with a razor blade. Make sure the edges are pasted down securely. Check the edges of all cutouts before going on to finish the project.

FINISHING: THE FINALE

The purpose of finishing decoupage with many coats of varnish, lacquer or water-soluble coating is to give it a deeply mellow, dimensional and—except in the case of contemporary decoupage—an antique look. Varnish gives the most luxurious and permanent finish, but is very slow-drying. Each coat must be allowed to dry for twenty-four hours. Lacquer is also long-lasting, and successive coats can be applied more rapidly than varnish. But lac-

quer has a tendency to chip off, so is not recommended for boxes and other objects which will be handled frequently. Water-soluble coatings can be applied very rapidly—as many as five or six coats in a day—and do not change the coloring of the cutouts. But they result in a softer finish, so three coats of varnish should be applied over them.

Wipe the surface of your project with a tack rag or lint-free cloth before applying the finish and between the successive coats. Apply ten coats of the finish you're using, letting one coat dry thoroughly before applying the next. Then wet-sand the surface with soapy water, using #400 wet-or-dry sandpaper and liquid detergent, and working back and forth in the direction of the grain. Sand very gently over areas with cutouts, so you don't sand through to the paper. Wipe off any white residue with a damp cloth, then rinse off any remaining suds and dry thoroughly with a soft towel. Continue applying coats of finish, wet-sanding between every few coats, until you have built up the kind of finish desired. Cutouts of thick paper require more coats of finish than cutouts of thin paper. Since varnish shrinks as it cures, you may want to add a few extra coats to make sure the final result is what you have in mind.

All finishes must be applied in thin coats to avoid drips and runs. Start strokes in center of surface and brush outward toward edges.

Polishing is the final step. First rub project in one direction with a piece of #0000 steel wool. When all the shine has been removed, wash off the object and dry it, then rub with an old nylon stocking. Using a soft, lint-free cloth, apply a little white furniture wax, rubbing it into the surface. Then polish with a soft, clean cloth. The furniture wax adds extra protection as well as a satiny finish.

Cutouts, *without printing on the back, are repeated at the back of this book.*

DECOUPAGE IDEAS

These easy-to-duplicate examples of decoupage are from Miss Vanderbilt's collection.

Gift-wrap for a photo album: Cover with white Con-Tact, apply cutouts, endpaper, gold paper braid. Wrap with a layer of clear plastic.

Two delicious though non-edible eggs, above and left, are decorated with cutouts from classic French prints in the Victorian manner.

The simplest kind of decoupage gives two clear glass paperweights Victorian charm. An old print is pasted, facing up, to bottom surface of each one.

A Roman gladiator—under glass. Pearlize cardboard backing for a see-through paperweight; seal as usual and apply cutout from a classic black-and-white print.

Spray an inexpensive gilded tray with two coats of acrylic sealer and apply exotic-looking cutouts with an Oriental flavor. Finish with varnish—the more coats the better.

Pearlized white paint sponged on over two coats of flat black paint works wonders for a wooden tea caddy. Two coats of acrylic sealer come next—and off to the chariot races!

It was just another glass ginger jar—and look at it now! The backs of the cutouts were sealed before applying, then all the work done on inside of jar—including sealing entire inside surface, patting on two coats of black acrylic paint with a sponge and finishing off with two coats of varnish. Shopping information for materials and prints is on page 223.

GIFTED CUTOUTS

Loving Greeting

Cutouts, without printing on back, are repeated at the back of this book.

May true friends be around you

SMALL GIFTS OF LOVE

for Valentine presents and other special occasions

Starting here, a baker's dozen of delightful little gifts you can put your heart into making (and not much money). They're all embellished with the beautiful cutouts on pages 38 and 39 reproduced from Gloria Vanderbilt's collection.

For the tooth fairy, above, a tiny round box, only 1 ½" high, but big enough to treasure a small tooth until the fairy arrives, then hold the reward.

Pencil caddy is a practical small gift with a romantic look, thanks to old-fashioned cutouts and beaded paper braid.

Miniature treasure chest blooming with flower cutouts measures less than 3"—just big enough to hold a precious bauble.

Cosmetic caddy has a heart full of flowers, however you look at it—though only one of its three cutouts shows here.

Give her your gilt-edged heart—this charming
little mirror (larger than life-size here) will get the
message across! Paint the back of the heart cutout
black before pasting it on mirror; otherwise, the
white edge of the paper will be reflected.

Grandmother's gift
is a fabric-lined box
holding baby's first curl.
Decorating the cover—
an angel, of course!

The top of the round, fabric-lined box opposite is slightly convex. To apply one of the angel-head cutouts, cut into the cutout circle of paper from any point around the edge to the center before applying paste to the back. This makes it possible to mold the cutout to conform to the rounded shape of the lid as you apply it. The cut in the paper will show slightly, so color both edges and fill in the slight "crack" with a matching colored pencil. To line the bottom of the box with fabric, cut a strip of thin cardboard as wide as the depth of the box minus 1/16", and as long as the circumference. Wrap a strip of fabric around it and glue the edges to the back of the cardboard. Then glue the wrapped strip to the inside of the box. Cut a circle of cardboard just slightly smaller than the inside dimension of the box. Cut a circle of polyester batting slightly smaller than the cardboard and a second layer slightly smaller than the first. Glue to one side of the cardboard circle and wrap with fabric as before. Glue the padded circle to the floor of the box and *voilà!*—a downy-soft surface like the inside of a jeweler's box on which to place a bow-tied lock of baby's first hair.

Hand her a ring that's a dramatic 1⅝" in diameter, decorated with a square medallion. Great as a scarf clasp, too. Rings for her ears are 1" wooden circles with snap-on backs—perfect size for the flower-centered cutouts on pages 38–39.

Diminutive metal trays decorated with flower-framed cutouts and brushed with violet paint have many uses.

Hearts-and-flowers camouflage for a square tissue box: it's covered in dollhouse wallpaper, then decorated with cutouts. See page 223 for shopping information.

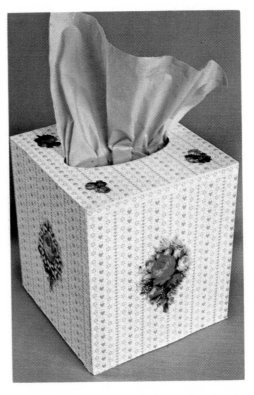

*T*ime to send a valentine! Make it a miniature grandfather's clock that really works, including the pendulum. Made-to-scale parts, including imported clock movement, come in a kit. Put it together, lacquer it black and apply miniature flower cutouts and gold paper braid.

Handy letter holder for the love notes you receive (or send) is appropriately decorated with two Victorian cutouts. As a valentine greeting, this black metal holder speaks for itself! Shopping information, page 223.

More pretty notes prove our valentine cutouts look charming on any pastel writing paper—not to mention plain white!

SEND
A LETTER
TO YOUR
LOVE

. . and write it on wildly romantic hot-pink-and-white notepaper made even more so by the addition of a charming heart and/or flower cutout from the collection shown on pages 38 and 39.

NEEDLEPOINT

GENERAL DIRECTIONS FOR WORKING NEEDLEPOINT

Very little special equipment is required for working needlepoint, but you should have everything you'll need on hand before you begin. In addition to canvas, yarn and a blunt tapestry needle, you'll need small embroidery scissors with narrow, pointed blades, which must be sharp. A metal thimble with deep indentations is useful, even though little pressure is needed to make a needlepoint stitch. A rectangular embroidery frame is helpful when working a large, heavy piece of needlepoint such as a rug, but is not necessary for smaller projects. A round frame or hoop used for other embroidery is not desirable for needlepoint because it will stretch the canvas. A blunt tapestry needle is always used for working needlepoint. Sizes of needles vary considerably; choose one with an eye just large enough to accommodate the yarn being used.

PREPARING THE CANVAS

Cut canvas 2″ larger on all sides than size indicated on chart. This 2″ margin is required for mounting the piece and remains unworked. Cut canvas in a square or rectangle even if working a circle or oval. Before beginning, bind raw edges with masking tape, adhesive tape or double-fold bias binding, or turn the raw edges under and whipstitch them to prevent raveling. The sides of the piece must be parallel to the selvedge edges of the canvas; mark the top of the piece with a colored thread to keep from turning it sideways inadvertently, and mark the center of each side edge as well.

WORKING WITH YARN

Cut strands of yarn (or embroidery floss) in 18″ lengths; never break it off, which stretches it. To thread the needle, double yarn over the end of the needle and slip it off, holding it tightly as close as possible to the fold. Push the flattened, folded end through the needle and pull the yarn through. To start, pull needle through the canvas from back to front, holding 1″ of yarn on back of canvas; cover this end with stitches as you proceed.

Be careful not to pull yarn too tightly as you work. Hold thumb on yarn near each stitch until you have pulled the yarn through the canvas, then remove thumb and pull yarn gently into place. Keep yarn from twisting by allowing needle and yarn to drop and untwist; working with twisted yarn will result in an uneven texture. When close to the end of a strand, fasten yarn by weaving through a few stitches on the back of the canvas; immediately trim the end to avoid tangles. Never knot the yarn. If you make a mistake, pluck out the yarn with the blunt end of the needle, or run the needle under the stitch (to protect the canvas) and snip yarn off close to the needle with embroidery scissors. Don't reuse pulled-out yarn. If working on a large piece without a frame, roll the canvas from the bottom up or from the top down and fasten with safety pins to make it easier to handle.

THE CONTINENTAL STITCH

The continental stitch is the most widely used needlepoint stitch and is used in most projects. (Where additional stitches are employed, diagrams and descriptions are given with the directions for the specific project.) Start at the upper right-hand corner of the canvas and work each row from right to left. When first row is completed, turn canvas upside down to work return row, continuing to work from right to left and keeping all stitches slanting in the same direction. Diagram 1 shows third row being worked; previous two rows are above it. Diagram 2 shows fourth row being worked; canvas has again been turned upside down and previous three rows are below it.

If you are left-handed, turn the diagrams upside down and start at the lower left corner of the canvas (instead of the upper right corner) and work from left to right.

HOW TO FOLLOW A CHART

Each square of the graph on which a chart is shown represents one stitch on the blank canvas. Each color used in the design is represented by a different symbol on the chart. A color key accompanies each chart, so it's easy to see which color is to be used for every stitch. Start at the upper right corner of the canvas and fill in the background to where the design begins. Then work the design area, following the chart, and fill in the background as you proceed. Fill in areas of one color as much as possible, working in rows. Single or scattered stitches in the same color are worked as they occur. When working a design which involves many colors, you'll find that keeping several needles threaded with different colors makes the work go much faster.

CLEANING AND BLOCKING

Try to keep your needlepoint clean as you work. It's a good idea to keep it in a plastic bag when not being worked on. If it needs a little freshening, brush over the surface with a clean cloth dipped in carbon tetrachloride or other cleaning fluid (do this only in a well-ventilated area).

After a piece is completely worked, it must be blocked to restore the original shape. Cover a soft wood surface with brown paper and mark the original size of the piece on the paper, keeping corners square. Place needlepoint right side down on marked outline and fasten with thumbtacks placed ½″ apart along the edges of the canvas. Wet thoroughly with a solution of one tablespoon salt to a quart of cold water and allow canvas to dry completely. If canvas is badly warped, repeat the process.

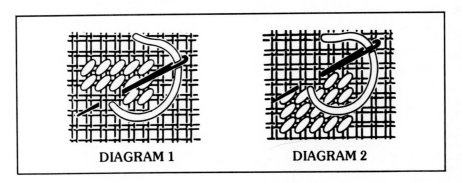

DIAGRAM 1   DIAGRAM 2

GROW
NEEDLEPOINT
VEGETABLES

Vibrant vegetables will thrive wherever—and however—you plant them . . . in cheerful check-bordered pillows, as pictures, as wall hangings or even brightening a carryall tote bag. They're worked in traditional continental stitch on 10-mesh-to-the-inch mono needlepoint canvas in clear, brilliant colors.

Velveteen cording in an accent color outlines each cushion and matches the backing. The same high-key shades could be used to frame the needlepoint pieces when used as pictures or wall plaques. They'd also look great decorating square wooden planters. You'll think of lots of other places to plant these tempting vegetables as you work them.

MATERIALS NEEDED
(for each 14″ x 14″ pillow)
  18″ x 18″ mono needlepoint canvas, 10-mesh-
     to-the-inch
  Brunsana Persian yarn in colors and approxi-
     mate amounts listed for each pillow
  ½ yard velveteen for back of pillow and cording
  1¾ yards cable cord, ¼″ diameter
  ½ yard muslin for pillow casing
  Polyester fiberfill for stuffing
  Thread to match fabric for back of pillow
  Tapestry needle
  Masking tape
  Thumbtacks
  Brown paper

All four pillows can be made from one yard of 36″-wide canvas.

Any upholstery-weight fabric can be used for back of pillow and to cover cording. We used velveteen in the following accent colors: Tomato pillow, orange; Radish pillow, hot pink; Cauliflower pillow, purple; Carrot pillow, green.

Read general directions for working needlepoint on page 48. On 18″ x 18″ piece of canvas for each pillow, mark outline of 14″ x 14″ finished pillow, allowing a 2″ margin on all sides. Bind raw edges with masking tape to prevent raveling.

Cut yarn into 18″ lengths. Work design in continental stitch, following needlepoint chart and color key for individual pillow. When needlepoint is complete, block according to directions on page 49 and trim margins to 1″.

Cut 16″ x 16″ piece of fabric for back of pillow. Cut remaining fabric into 1½″-wide bias strips. With right sides facing, seam strips together on the lengthwise grain to make strip long enough to go around edge of pillow with ½″ overlap. Press each seam as stitched, then press allowances open. Fold strip in half lengthwise, wrong sides together, and place cord in fold. Using adjustable cording or zipper foot, stitch close to cord along length of strip.

Stitch cording around right side of finished canvas, with raw edges of cording facing outward and stitching line directly over edge of needlepoint along sides, rounding corners slightly.

To join ends of cording, push covering on one end back and cut off ½″ of cord. Turn raw edge of covering ¼″ to inside and insert other end of cording; blindstitch ends of covering securely together along fold. Continue stitching cording in place.

Pin finished canvas and fabric together with right sides facing and edges even, enclosing cording. Stitch together 1″ from edges, crowding cording foot against cord and leaving an 8″ opening in the center of one side. Trim allowances to ½″ and clip canvas at corners. Turn to right side.

To make inner casing, cut two 16″ x 16″ pieces of muslin. With right sides facing, stitch together ½″ from edges, leaving a 6″ opening in center of one side. Turn casing to right side and stuff plumply with fiberfill. Turn edges of opening to inside and slipstitch opening closed. Insert inner pillow into embroidered pillow cover. Stuff corners with additional fiberfill if necessary. Turn edges of fabric and canvas along opening to inside and slipstitch opening closed.

TOMATO PILLOW 14″ × 14″

Color		Brunsana Persian Yarn #	Yards	Color		Brunsana Persian Yarn #	Yards
☐	Pure white	41	150	☒	Maroon	80	15
⊙	Light tangerine	118	2	⊡	Avocado	32	13
▨	Deep tangerine	4	30	◪	Holly green	205	6
▣	Bright red	82	80	⊞	Dark juniper	248	6

RADISH PILLOW 14″ × 14″

Color		Brunsana Persian Yarn #	Yards	Color		Brunsana Persian Yarn #	Yards
□	Pure white	41	165	☒	Medium green	24	7
☒	Pale hot pink	276	6	⊞	Shamrock	23	12
◪	Medium rose	125	60	⊟	Pale gold	3	1
⊡	Maroon	80	24	⊙	Pecan	266	1
⊡	Bright green	26	23	◪	Purple	219	3

CAULIFLOWER PILLOW 14″ × 14″

Color		Brunsana Persian Yarn #	Yards
□	Pure white	41	150
◪	Light green	28	60
⊡	Bright green	26	66

Color		Brunsana Persian Yarn #	Yards
⊞	Shamrock	23	18
⊠	Light plum	135	6

CARROT PILLOW 14″ × 14″

Color		Brunsana Persian Yarn #	Yards
☐	Pure white	41	165
⊡	Bright green	26	25
Ⓥ	Medium green	24	6
⊞	Shamrock	23	6
⊠	Dark tiger	228	8

Color		Brunsana Persian Yarn #	Yards
◩	Orange	5	75
⊙	Dark bittersweet	269	25
⊟	Pale gold	3	1
◎	Pecan	266	1

TULIP-TIME
TRIPTYCH

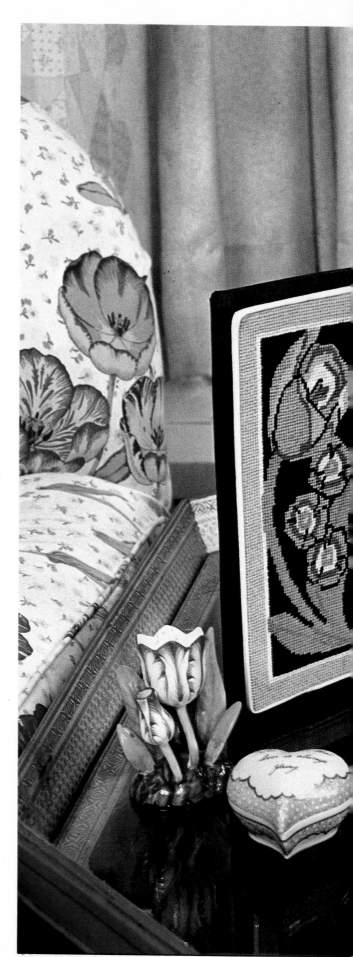

One of Gloria's favorite flowers is the tulip, and an extensive collection of graceful, tulip-shaped vases in antique English porcelain blooms all year round in her objet-filled apartment. They inspired the free-form beauties that bloom here in a striking triptych—their flowing forms worked in six-strand embroidery floss in subtle gradations of color. Three separate pieces of needlepoint are mounted on pieces of cardboard and then on fabric-covered foamcore boards. The trio of panels could also be framed to hang as pictures.

Read general directions on page 48 before beginning needlepoint. Use 14-mesh-to-the-inch canvas and D.M.C six-strand embroidery floss in colors listed in color key. Be sure to cut each piece of canvas 2″ larger all around than size indicated by chart. Using full six strands of floss, work needlepoint designs in continental stitch and block finished pieces. When dry, trim margins of canvas to 1″ on all sides.

To mount needlepoint pieces to form triptych, you'll need three pieces of mounting cardboard in same sizes as needlepoint; three pieces of foamcore board, each ½″ larger all around than needlepoint and cardboard; 2¾ yards of white cotton cording, ¼″ in diameter; ¾ yard black polished cotton fabric, 36″ wide; ½ yard fusible webbing; all-purpose glue.

Place each blocked piece of needlepoint on cardboard of matching size. Stretch unworked margins of canvas around edges of cardboard and hold in place by pushing straight pins through canvas and partway into back edges of cardboard; place pins about 1″ apart. Check needlepoint to make sure rows are straight, then carefully hammer pins into cardboard the rest of the way. Using a large-eyed needle and carpet thread, lace raw edges of canvas together over back of cardboard to hold it taut; lace across width, then length, mitering cor-

ners as you lace. To edge needlepoint with white cording, cut cording 1″ longer than perimeter of cardboard. Apply glue to edges of cardboard and press cording in place along edges, with ends meeting at center of bottom edge.

To join ends of cording, push casing at one end back and cut off ½″ of cord; turn raw edge of casing ¼″ to inside. Insert other end of cording into open end of casing and slip-stitch turned edge of casing in place. Cut a piece of black fabric 2″ larger all around than each piece of foamcore board. Ap-

ply glue to one side of board and center glued side on wrong side of fabric. Smooth fabric against board; allow glue to dry. Pull excess fabric around edges of board and glue to back. Center each mounted needlepoint piece on fabric-covered board; glue in place. Panels are glued to a double layer of black fabric, which finishes the back and hinges the panels together. From black fabric, cut a piece 20¼″ wide x 22″ long. From fusing material, cut a piece 20¼″ x 11″. With right sides together, fold fabric in half horizontally; press fold. Place fus-

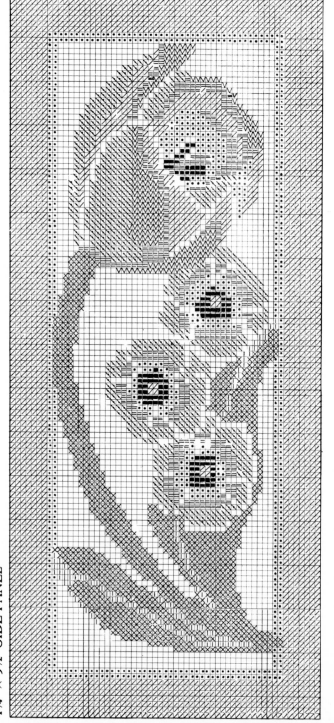

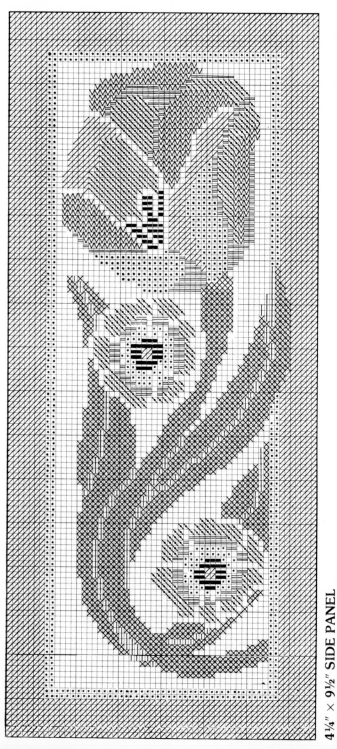

4¼″ × 9½″ SIDE PANEL

4¼″ × 9½″ SIDE PANEL

ing material over folded fabric; stitch ½″ from raw edges along three sides, leaving a 4″ opening along long edge. Trim seams and turn right side out. Turn raw edges to inside; slipstitch opening closed. To fuse the two layers of fabric together, press according to manufacturer's directions. Center largest needlepoint panel over black fabric; tape in place. Place each side panel ⅛″ from center panel, aligning top and bottom edges. Edges of panels should extend ⅛″. Check to make sure panels align; glue firmly in place.

Color		D.M.C Number	Skeins
☑	Yellow	743	7
☐	Black	—	6
⊡	White	—	3
☱	Violet	208	2
☑	Lilac	211	2
◩	Peach	758	3
▢	Lime green	906	1
☒	Medium green	912	4
▥	Dark green	910	2

8″ × 9½″ CENTER PANEL

"PANSIES" PILLOW

Miss Vanderbilt's charming collage, titled simply "Pansies," inspired this equally charming pillow. The nosegay motif, complete with lacy white doily, is worked in needlepoint, and makes an ideal design for a decorative round pillow. Violet-and-white checked gingham is used twice in the collage, and used here on the bias for the unusual gathered boxing, as well as the back of the pillow. You can make the pillow and the collage, too. Directions for the pillow are right here; directions for the collage are on page 20.

Before starting needlepoint, read general directions on page 48. Use 12-mesh-to-the-inch canvas cut in a 14″ square. Use three-ply Persian yarn separated into two-ply lengths. Color key lists number of yards required after separating yarn.

Worked circle of needlepoint is 10″ in diameter. Using a compass, mark a 10″-diameter circle in center of canvas. Circle is shown only partially on chart. Area between white doily and completed circle is the same violet as background.

Following chart and color key, work background and design in continental stitch. Block completed piece following directions on page 49. When dry, trim canvas to 1″ beyond marked circle.

Directions follow for completing the pillow cover and making the inner pillow.

ROUND COVER FOR
NEEDLEPOINT PILLOW

MATERIALS NEEDED
(To complete needlepoint pillow cover and make inner pillow)
- 1 yard checked gingham fabric
- ½ yard muslin for inner casing
- ½ yard cable cord, ¼" diameter
- ½ pound polyester fiberfill for stuffing

From muslin, cut two 11½"-diameter circles and enough 2½"-wide bias strips to make a 32"-long boxing strip when stitched together. Stitch one edge of boxing strip to one muslin circle, ½" from raw edges; stitch other edge of boxing to remaining muslin circle, leaving a 3" opening. Turn muslin casing to right side and stuff tautly with fiberfill; slipstitch opening closed.

From checked fabric, cut two bias strips 1½" wide x 33" long to cover cord; cut enough 2½"-wide bias strips to make 80"-long boxing strip. Cut strips for cording first, from center of fabric, so each one will have to be seamed only once. Cut a 10½"-diameter circle from remainder of checked fabric. Center a 33"-length of cord on wrong side of each 1½"-wide bias strip and cover cord.

Gather both long edges of boxing strip to 32" length. With raw edges together, and with cording extending ½" beyond boxing at each end, stitch one strip of cording to each long edge of boxing on right side of fabric, following stitching line of cording. With right sides together, baste corded boxing strip to embroidered circle, keeping cording along edge of needlepoint, and overlapping ends of cording ½". To join ends, pull cord out of covering on one end and cut off ½" of cord. Turn raw edge of covering in ¼". Insert other end of cording into open end of covering and slipstitch covering closed. Stitch boxing to circle. With right sides together, stitch other edge of boxing to circle of checked fabric, leaving a 6" opening. Turn cover to right side and insert muslin pillow; slipstitch opening closed.

Needlepoint design
is centered in
10″-diameter circle.

Color Key

	Color	Yards		Color	Yards		Color	Yards
Ⓢ	Light red-violet	2	⊻	Mauve	3	◨	Blue	2
◩	Red-violet	6	◪	Bright yellow	10	◪	Light blue	2
☐	Violet	40	◫	Pale yellow	10	⊟	Pink	4
◪	Purple	10	⊠	Light green	4	⊡	White	16
⊞	Dark purple	2	◿	Green	12			
⊟	Lavender	6	◼	Dark green	6			

RECAPTURE THE 20'S WITH CLARENCE AND CLAUDETTE

*O*ur *cloche-capped flapper and her top-hatted swain are immortalized in needlepoint—capturing forever the glamour of an era when hearts were young and gay. Debonair Clarence and ultra-chic Claudette are dressed to the nines, ready to dance the night away. They're done in a combination of continental and gobelin stitches for interesting*

Read general directions on page 48 before beginning needlepoint. "Clarence" and "Claudette" are worked on 14-mesh-to-the-inch mono canvas in a combination of continental stitch and gobelin stitch, using Brunsana three-ply Persian yarn, D.M.C six-strand embroidery floss and Veloura one-strand velvet thread. The color key lists the amounts needed for each portrait.

To work continental stitch, follow instructions and diagram on page 49. To work gobelin stitch, see diagram on page 73. To cover an area with gobelin stitch, work the row with upright vertical stitches from left to right, going over the number of meshes required to make stitch the desired length. Work second row of stitches directly below first row, going from right to left. When working gobelin stitch, keep yarn flat and untwisted, employing a little less tension than usual, so rows of stitches will have a slightly rounded or quilted look. The gobelin stitch is usually worked in rows of equal-length stitches, but in this case, the length of stitches in some rows varies to follow the design lines of the portraits. Always work the stitch in upright position; to work horizontal rows, simply turn the canvas.

The needlepoint charts on pages 68–69 indicate both the stitch and the color to be used. The eyes, cheeks, brows, lashes and lips are all worked in continental stitch; the colors are indicated by symbols that refer to the color key. Actual color numbers are given for all other areas. The letter C after a number means that area is worked in continental stitch; all remaining areas are worked in gobelin stitch. Directional lines within these areas indicate either vertical or horizontal gobelin stitches and also the length of the stitches. Where large areas of striped background or hair are all one color, only one number is given for entire area.

When working the continental stitch, use two-ply Persian yarn or eight-ply embroidery floss; when working the gobelin stitch, use three-ply Persian yarn, eight-ply embroidery floss or one-ply velvet thread. (Add two strands to the standard six-strand embroidery floss.)

Cut canvas and bind edges as described in general directions. Following needlepoint chart, count down from center top of canvas to first row of forehead. Work face, neck, shoulders and head, finishing continental stitch first. Then work background areas and border. Block finished needlepoint, following directions on page 49.

dimension, and in a mixture of Persian yarn, embroidery floss and velvet thread for contrast in textures. If you or someone on your gift list is enamored of F. Scott Fitzgerald and the whole 1920's scene, Clarence and Claudette would be ideal companions.

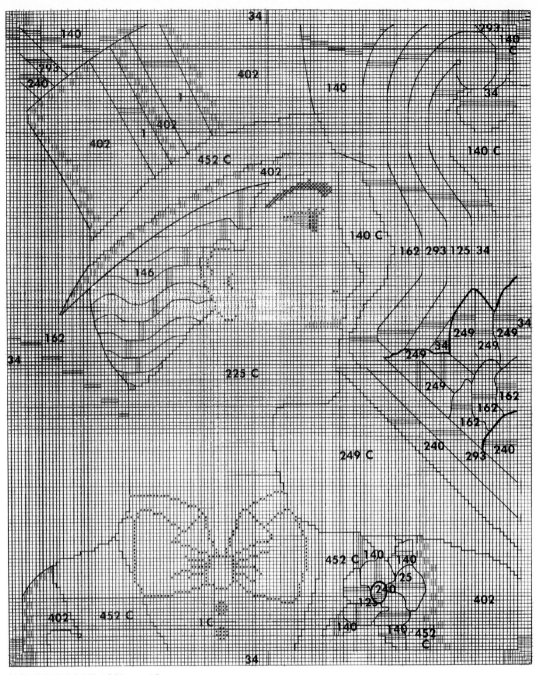

"CLARENCE" 10¾″ × 13″

COLOR KEY   = Clarence   = Claudette

	Color	Brunsana Persian Yarn	Yards (Clarence)	Yards (Claudette)	D.M.C Embroidery Floss	Skeins (Clarence)	Skeins (Claudette)
⊙	Medium aqua	162	30	30	809	1	1
	Medium juniper	249	22	22			
	Deep amber	293	7	10			
	Lemon	240	4	10			
	Medium rose	125	5	4			
·	Rose	94		4	957		1

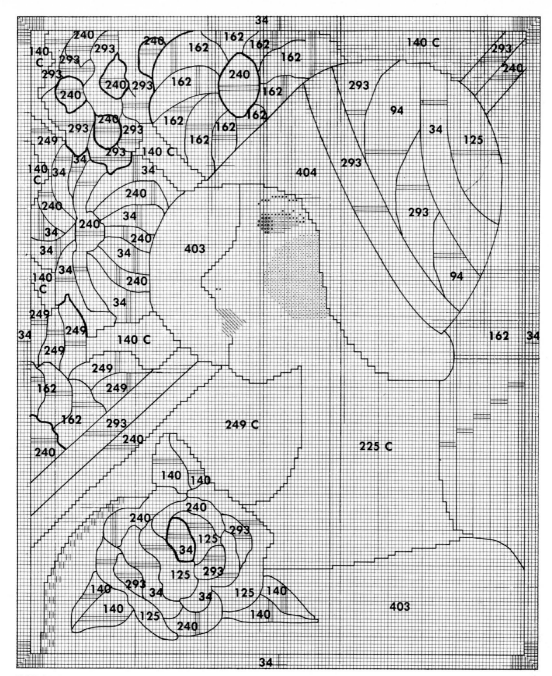

"CLAUDETTE" 10¾" × 13"

Color	D.M.C Embroidery Floss	Skeins	Skeins	Veloura Velvet Thread	Skeins	Skeins
White	34	14	20			
Dark azure	140	16	12			
⊠ Tobacco	146	7				
⊟ Snow white	1	3	1			
Flesh	225	5	4			
⊡ Black	310	1	1	402	2	
⧄ Bright rose	350		1	404		1
⊞ Pale pink	758	1				
Grey	452	2				
Maroon				403		1

"PAINT" A NEEDLEPOINT BOUQUET

You know what a beautiful bowl of fresh flowers does for a room. They add life and color and a welcome touch of springtime whatever the season. Having the real thing always at hand may be hard to manage, but you can "paint" a lovely needlepoint bouquet that will never wilt. And you needn't spend a whole season doing it. The pretty bouquet here, worked in a palette of bright and lively pastels, is done entirely in gobelin stitch, which goes comparatively quickly, even if you're a novice at needlepoint. This "painting" was worked on 12-mesh-to-the-inch mono needlepoint canvas, using wool tapestry yarn.

Obviously, your finished "painting" of spring-blooming flowers will make a stunning picture—even in a very simple frame. But why not display your artwork a little more imaginatively? Just one way to do so is sketched here. Frame your "painting" in a good-looking tray—wicker or whatever—and cover it with glass for a real conversation piece.

MATERIALS NEEDED
16¾" x 20½" mono needlepoint canvas, 12-mesh-to-the-inch

D.M.C wool tapestry yarn in following colors:
  #7852 Pink, 14 yards
  #7799 Pale blue, 52 yards
  #7850 Coral, 14 yards
  #7742 Orange, 18 yards
  #7431 Yellow, 10 yards
  #7549 Light Olive, 20 yards
  #7547 Olive, 20 yards
  #7342 Green, 20 yards
  Blanc (White), 65 yards
Masking tape
Tapestry needle
Thumbtacks
Brown Paper

Read general directions for working needlepoint on page 48 before beginning project.

Mark 12¾" x 16½" outline of finished needlepoint picture on canvas, leaving a 2" margin on all sides. Bind raw edges with masking tape to prevent raveling.

Cut yarn into 18" lengths. Following chart, work entire design in gobelin stitch. Directional line within each marked area indicates either vertical or

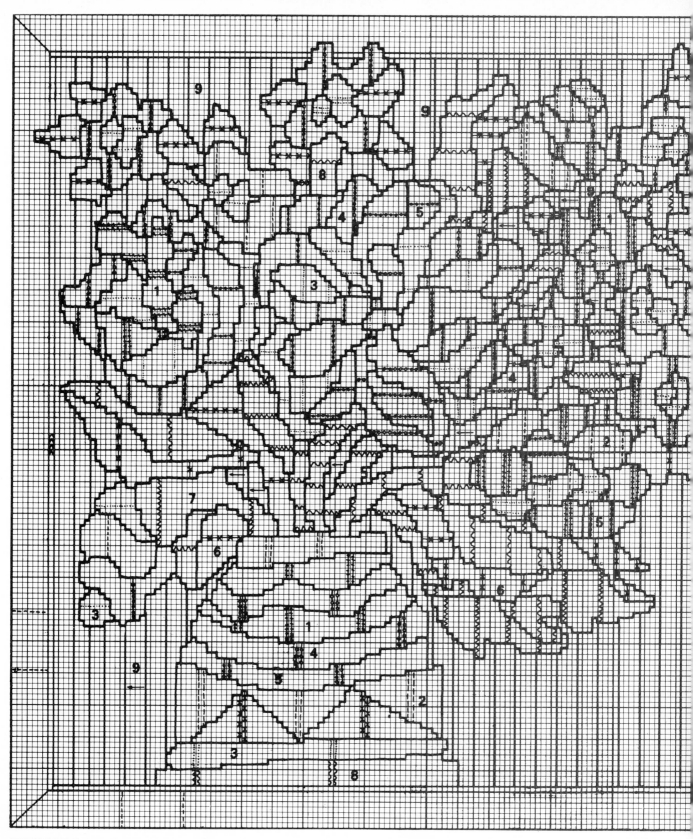

NEEDLEPOINT "PAINTING" 12¾″ × 16½″

	COLOR KEY			Color	D.M.C Tapestry Yarn			Color	D.M.C Tapestry Yarn
		1	┼┼┼	Pink	#7852	4	─o─o─o─	Orange	#7742
		2	- - - - -	Pale blue	#7799	5	─•─•─•─	Yellow	#7431
		3	··············	Coral	#7850	6	✕✕✕	Light olive	#7549

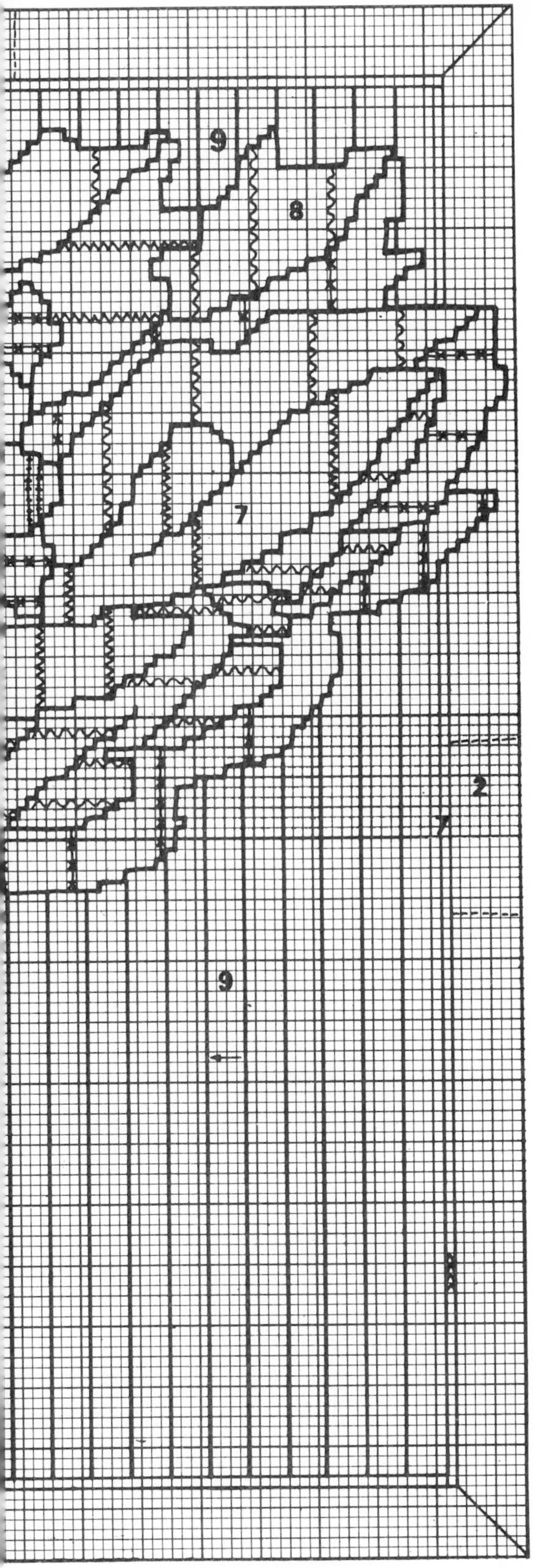

		Color	D.M.C Tapestry Yarn
7	∧∧∧∧∧∧	Olive	#7547
8	∿∿∿∿	Green	#7342
9	←	White	Blanc

horizontal gobelin stitches and the length of stitch at that point; the symbols used in directional lines refer to the color key. To make color identification even easier, the colors are also numbered in color key, with numbers (as well as symbols) shown in sample areas of chart as a double reference.

Each square of graph on which chart is shown represents one mesh hole of canvas. Follow chart to determine how many meshes to go over for each stitch; refer to color key for color to be used. Entire white background is worked horizontally.

When needlepoint is complete, block piece as directed on page 49.

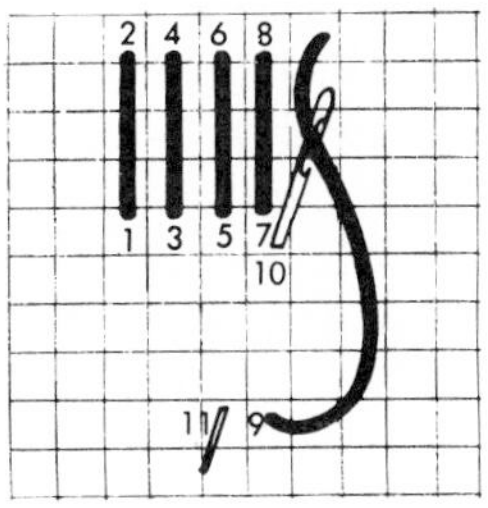

GOBELIN STITCH

To cover an area with gobelin stitch, work the row with upright vertical stitches from left to right, going over the number of meshes required to make stitch the desired length. Work second row of stitches directly below first row, going from right to left. Keep yarn flat and untwisted, employing a little less tension than usual so rows of stitches will have a slightly rounded or quilted look. To work horizontal rows, simply turn the canvas.

NEEDLEPOINT MINIATURES TO COMBINE MANY WAYS

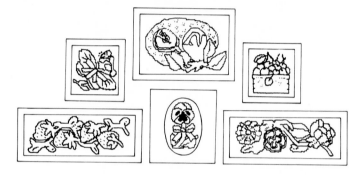

Gloria Vanderbilt's penchant for putting unexpected elements together inspired this whimsical assemblage of charming but unrelated motifs—for you to arrange as you please. The varied shapes and sizes of the miniature needlepoint pictures fit together in an amazing number of ways.

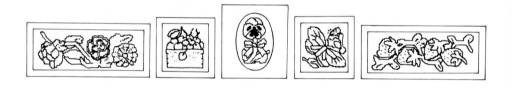

No, it isn't a game. Well . . . yes it is, in a way. The six groups of little sketches show just a few of the ways you can arrange the needlepoint miniatures shown in color. Each one is a mini-masterpiece of needlepoint design, and once you start rearranging them, you won't be able to stop. (It really *is* a fascinating game.) Note that the strawberries and flowers can be used horizontally or vertically—or even upside down! We show the strawberries growing *up* in the photograph, and the flowers growing both ways in the sketches. Make all six designs or as many as you like. We ran out of space before getting around to possible arrangements of three, four or five of them. You could make three for a start and enjoy a mini-arrangement while completing the rest—revising the arrangement as you finish each new one. And how about that idea for a double-barreled gift? Make three or four for an upcoming birthday or anniversary, and complete the whole works in time for Christmas. Double the fun by keeping the finale a surprise when you proudly present the first installment!

We used D.M.C six-strand embroidery floss on 14-to-the-inch canvas, and cut narrow mats to match the pale beige backgrounds to make framing optional. Charts for all six designs follow; directions for working the continental stitch used in all are on page 49. Each square of the graph on which a chart is shown represents one stitch on the blank canvas. A color key is included with the charts; a different symbol represents each color used in the design. Follow the chart, consulting the color key, and you can't go wrong!

Read general directions for working in needlepoint on page 48 before beginning. Use 14-mesh-to-the-inch canvas and D.M.C six-strand embroidery floss in colors listed in color key below. The number of skeins needed for all six miniatures is listed with color key.

Cut canvas for each miniature 2″ larger on all sides than size indicated by chart and bind raw edges of canvas to prevent raveling. Outside dimensions of each piece are also outside dimensions of its mat. Mats shown in photograph are ⁹⁄₁₆″ wide, including bevels.

Miniatures are worked in continental stitch. Block each piece and mount on cardboard cut to same size as worked needlepoint. Tape unworked edges to back of cardboard, and glue mat to needlepoint. Glue narrow velvet ribbon around edges or frame if desired.

COLOR KEY

	Color	D.M.C Number	Skeins
☐	Ecru	—	11
☑	Yellow	726	2
◩	Yellow-gold	725	1
☒	Gold	783	1
⊞	Yellow-green	3347	1
☑	Lime green	704	1
⊟	Medium green	913	1
⊞	Dark green	911	2
⊡	French blue	809	2
⊡	Pink	957	1
⊟	Red	350	2
⊙	Black	—	4

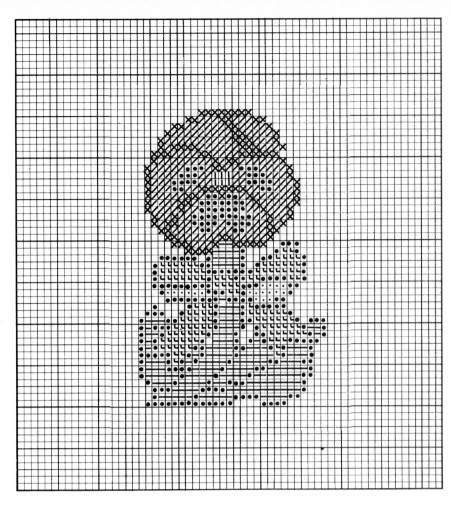

PANSY 4¹⁵⁄₁₆″ × 4⁷⁄₁₆″

PEARS 4⁷⁄₈″ × 6⁷⁄₈″

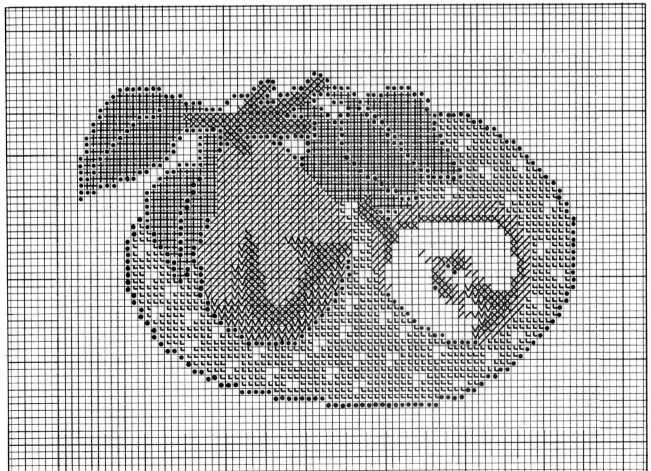

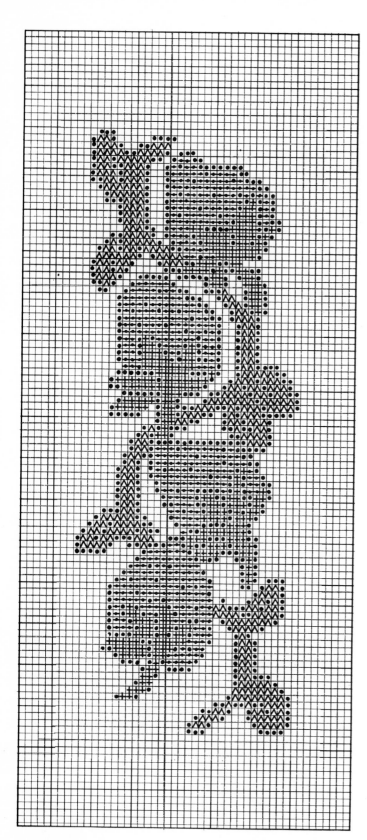

STRAWBERRIES 8¼″ × 3½″

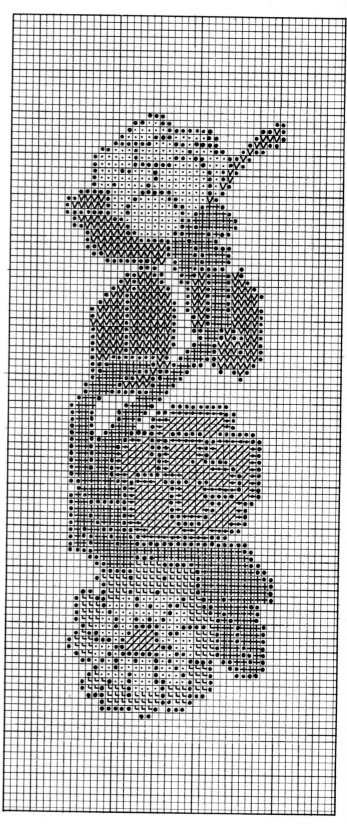

FLOWERS 8¼″ × 3⁷⁄₁₆″

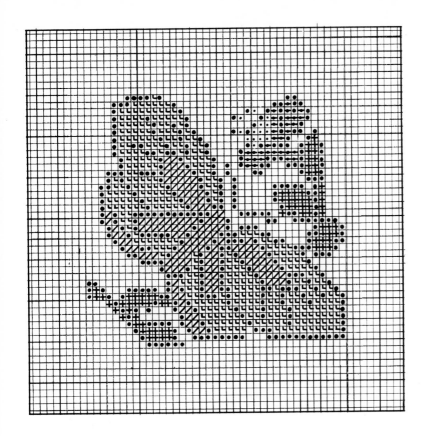

BUTTERFLY 4¹⁄₁₆″ × 4¹⁄₁₆″

BASKET OF CHERRIES 4¹⁄₁₆″ × 4¹⁄₁₆″

COLOR KEY

	Color	D.M.C Number	Skeins
☐	Ecru	—	11
◪	Yellow	726	2
◲	Yellow-gold	725	1
⊠	Gold	783	1
⊞	Yellow-green	3347	1
☑	Lime green	704	1
⊟	Medium green	913	1
⊞	Dark green	911	2
⊡	French blue	809	2
⊡	Pink	957	1
⊟	Red	350	2
⊙	Black	—	4

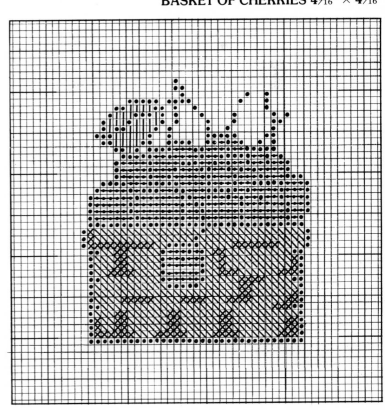

TRADITIONAL GREEK TAPESTRY TRANSLATED INTO NEEDLEPOINT

If you've ever visited the Aegean Islands, you'll probably recognize this stylized pattern of tulips and poppies used as a repeat motif and border design. It's typical of the way flower forms are interpreted in Greek tapestry, and translates beautifully into a needlepoint pattern for an area rug—in a choice of two different sizes. Notice in the diagram that accompanies the directions, the ingenious way the border design changes directions at the corners. The same pattern could easily be adapted for a pillow.

Materials Needed
(see yardage table for amounts and colors)
    Double-mesh needlepoint canvas,
        10-mesh-to-the-inch
    Paternayan Persian wool yarn
    Heavy-duty burlap
    Carpet thread
    Tapestry needle

Before beginning needlepoint, read general directions on page 48. Rug shown in photograph is 5'6" x 8'; design can also be used for small area-size rug. Yardage table gives dimensions of canvas and burlap required for both sizes; it also indicates number of center motifs in each size, and includes amount of yarn needed for all motifs, borders and background.

The chart for working needlepoint shows one corner of rug, including three borders and one center motif. The corner diagonally opposite the one shown in chart matches it; the other two corners are like the one shown in the photograph. This slight change is necessary because the large flower motifs in Border #2 are directional. Sketch showing placement of large motifs on small rug illustrates this; corners of large rug are worked the same way. In large rug, center motif is repeated eleven times across the width of rug and seventeen times down length of rug.

Allowing 2" margin on all sides, mark outer edge of area to be worked on canvas. If two pieces of canvas must be joined to make rug desired size, determine line where pattern will be joined. Cut each piece of canvas 2" beyond joining line. Work needlepoint to within 2" of joining line on each piece. Trim 2" margins of unworked canvas to 1" beyond joining line. Overlap edges of canvas so

BORDER #3   BORDER #2   BORDER #1

COLOR KEY	Color	Paternayan Number	Color	Paternayan Number
☒	Blue	752	☑ Pale green	542
⧄	Pale blue	743	◢ Russet	269
·	Yellow	452	☐ Beige	012
■	Green	530		

one joining line is directly on top of other and meshes match; hold in place with large T pins through both pieces of canvas. Finish working design through both pieces of canvas.

Mark off 1¾" or 17 meshes for Border #1; mark off 3¼" or 33 meshes for Border #2; mark off 1¼" or 13 meshes for Border #3. Mark squares for center motifs 4⅞" or 49 meshes square. Then mark the center of each side of rug. Flower and leaf motifs in Border #1 and Border #3 reverse direction at this center point on each side. Work the design within these borders from each corner toward the center, where the motifs meet.

Rug shown is worked entirely in a variation of the continental stitch, in which the direction of the stitches alternates in each row, producing a herringbone effect. See Diagram 1. However, the entire rug may be worked in regular continental stitch if desired. See page 49 for diagrams illustrating continental stitch. Follow chart and color key to work design.

Begin working at upper right corner of canvas and work the center motifs first. Then work Borders #3, #2 and #1 in that order. Fill in background last. See general directions on page 49 for blocking instructions.

To finish rug, turn unworked margins plus first row of needlepoint to wrong side; catch-stitch to back of rug, folding canvas at corners to form miter. Turn 2⅛" margin along all edges of burlap to wrong side and baste in place. Pin burlap to wrong side of rug, butting turned edges against first row of needlepoint. Slipstitch in place, just catching needlepoint in stitches.

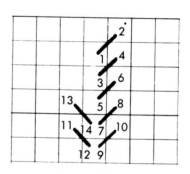

DIAGRAM 1

YARDAGE TABLE

Finished Size	Size of Canvas and Burlap	Number of Center Motifs	(Yarn Requirements Given in Yards)						
			Blue	Pale Blue	Yellow	Green	Pale Green	Russet	Beige
5'6" x 8' (66" x 96")	5'10" x 8'4" (70" x 100")	187	2,212	784	681	591	927	181	3,127
3' x 4' (36" x 48")	3'4" x 4'4" (40" x 52")	35	612	146	200	131	213	47	766

AFGHANS

An afghan? What a sedate word to describe such a blaze of pattern and color! And doesn't it look exactly like Gloria? She might have designed the flower motifs herself—and mixed the color combinations on her own palette. It usually reposes in her multipatterned living room, tossed with artful casualness across a chaise. But she often moves it around. "I love the unusual combinations of colors," she comments. "Bring it into any room and that room immediately begins to sparkle." It's crocheted in strips of 4½" squares and then embroidered. The strips are joined together on the diagonal, which gives it its intriguing zigzag outline. There are 154 squares in all, and thirteen different flower motifs. But no two squares are exactly alike. The background colors are repeated at random; the cross-stitch motifs pick up the same colors in endless combinations. Follow the colors in the photo or mix your own.

GLORIA'S
FAVORITE AFGHAN
GLOWS WITH
TWO TECHNIQUES

MATERIALS NEEDED

Worsted-weight knitting yarn, a total of about 70 ounces in various colors, for crocheted squares and embroidery

10 ounces black yarn for joining and edging

Afghan hook, size F

Crochet hook, size F

Tapestry needles

Afghan is 58″ x 72″ and is made of 16 diagonal strips of various lengths composed of crocheted squares. There are 154 squares in all, each approximately 4½″ x 4½″ (19 ribs high and 20 vertical bars wide).

Diagram 1 shows layout of squares and strips. Heavy black lines indicate crocheted joinings and edging. Numeral within each square indicates background color, as listed in color key. Arrangement of colors is random, so you can follow original color placement or substitute your own colors and arrangement.

Crochet Abbreviations and Stitches

beg = beginning
ch = chain
dc = double crochet
lp = loop
p = picot
rnd = round
sc = single crochet
sk = skip
sl st = slipstitch
sp = space
st = stitch
tog = together
tr = treble crochet
yo = yarn over

* (asterisk): repeat directions following * as many extra times as directed. "*2 dc in next st, 1 dc in next st, repeat from * 4 times" means to work directions after first * until second * is reached, then go back to first * 4 times more. Work 5 times in all.

Picot: To make a picot, ch 3, 4 or required number, sc or sl st in first st of ch.

Slipstitch: Insert hook through st, catch yarn and, with one motion, draw through both the st and the one lp on hook. The sl st is used for joining.

GAUGE: 5 sts = 1″; 9 rows = 2″.

AFGHAN STITCH: With afghan hook, ch 22.

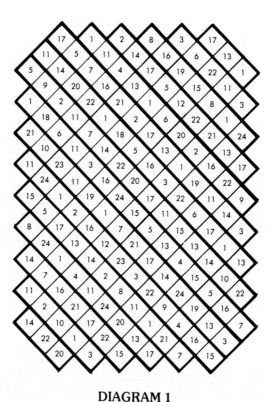

DIAGRAM 1

COLOR KEY

1 Gold	13 Aqua
2 Bright red	14 Pale beige
3 Cranberry	15 Beige
4 Maroon	16 Pale yellow
5 Shrimp pink	17 Dark brown
6 Bright pink	18 Brown
7 Dark green	19 Purple
8 Green	20 Lavender
9 Light olive	21 Mauve pink
10 Dark olive	22 Orange
11 Pale blue	23 Marigold
12 Bright blue	24 Coral

Row 1: Keeping all lps on hook, pull up a lp in second ch from hook and in each ch across—22 lps (Diagram 2).

DIAGRAM 2

To work lps off: Yo hook, pull through first lp, * yo hook, pull through next 2 lps, repeat from * across until 1 lp remains (Diagram 3). Lp that remains on hook always counts as first st of next row.

DIAGRAM 3

Row 2: Keeping all lps on hook, sk first vertical bar (lp on hook is first st), pull up a lp under next vertical bar and under each vertical bar across to last st (Diagram 4), insert hook under last vertical bar and in lp at back of bar, pull up a lp. Work lps off as before. Repeat row 2 for afghan stitch.

DIAGRAM 4

TO WORK AFGHAN: For first strip of 3 squares, using afghan hook, ch 22. Work in afghan stitch for 19 rows to complete first square. Change color by working off last 2 lps of 19th row with new color.

With new color, work 19 rows. Change to third color, work 19 rows to complete third square. Sl st in second vertical bar and in each vertical bar across. End off.

Work second strip as for first strip, making strip 5 squares long. Work third strip 7 squares long, fourth strip 9 squares long, fifth strip 11 squares long, sixth strip 13 squares long, seventh strip 14 squares long, eighth strip 15 squares long, ninth strip 15 squares long, tenth strip 14 squares long, eleventh strip 13 squares long, twelfth strip 11 squares long, thirteenth strip 9 squares long, fourteenth strip 7 squares long, fifteenth strip 5 squares long, sixteenth strip 3 squares long.

Edging for strips: With black yarn and crochet hook, work 1 rnd of sc around each strip, making 1 sc in each sl st across top of strip, 1 sc in side of each row, 1 sc in each ch at bottom of strip and 3 sc in each corner st. Sl st in first sc. End off.

Embroider strips, following directions for embroidery.

TO WORK EMBROIDERY: Thirteen different flower motifs are embroidered on crocheted squares of afghan. Heavy broken lines on embroidery charts indicate backstitch; small leaflike blossoms on Chart B are worked in lazy-daisy stitch. Otherwise, cross-stitch is used throughout, and symbols employed in charts represent changes of color (only) within each motif. The thirteen motifs are used at random and each is worked in a variety of color schemes, using the background colors in different combinations. See photograph for placement of motifs (on most of afghan) or arrange the motifs to suit yourself, making sure the same motif is not repeated within a small area.

Leaving 1 stitch for seaming at each side of strip, follow charts to embroider designs (actual strip is 22 stitches wide; chart shows 20). Use one 18″ strand of yarn in needle and begin working cross-stitch motifs, making one cross-stitch over vertical bar of 1 afghan stitch (Diagram 5). Heavy broken

Cross-Stitch on Afghan Stitch

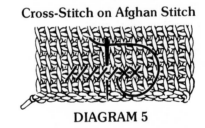

DIAGRAM 5

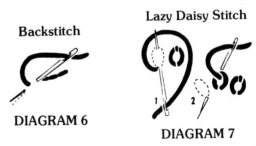

Backstitch

DIAGRAM 6

Lazy Daisy Stitch

DIAGRAM 7

lines on Charts B, J, K, L and M are worked in backstitch (Diagram 6); these stitches are worked over afghan stitch in the direction indicated on charts. Leaflike blossoms indicated on Chart B are worked in lazy-daisy stitch (Diagram 7). Embroider all strips before joining.

To join strips: Hold two strips, wrong sides tog, lining up squares evenly. From right side, using black yarn, sc strips tog where they touch, working through both strands of each sc on both strips. Join strips as follows: Center first strip on second strip, second strip on third strip, etc., to sixth strip. Place top of seventh strip and eighth strip even with top of sixth strip. Beginning with ninth strip, start each strip one square down from top.

FINISHING: Run in yarn ends on wrong side.

Edging: Using black yarn and crochet hook, work 1 rnd sc around entire edge of afghan, working 3 sc in each outer corner and skipping 1 st at each inner corner. Join in first sc.

Next Rnd: Ch 1, * sc in each of next 3 sc, ch 3, sc in third ch from hook for p, sk 1 sc, repeat from * around, skipping an extra st at inner corners and working extra sts at outer corners to keep work flat. Join; end off.

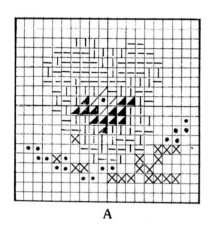

A

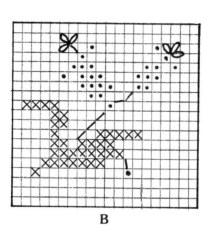

B

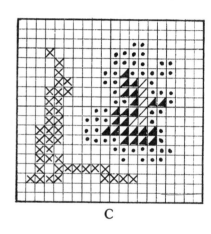

C

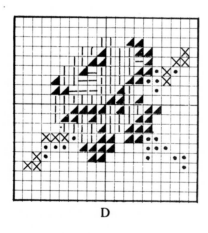

D

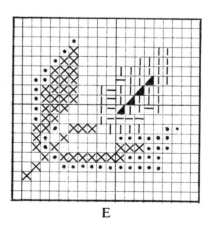

E

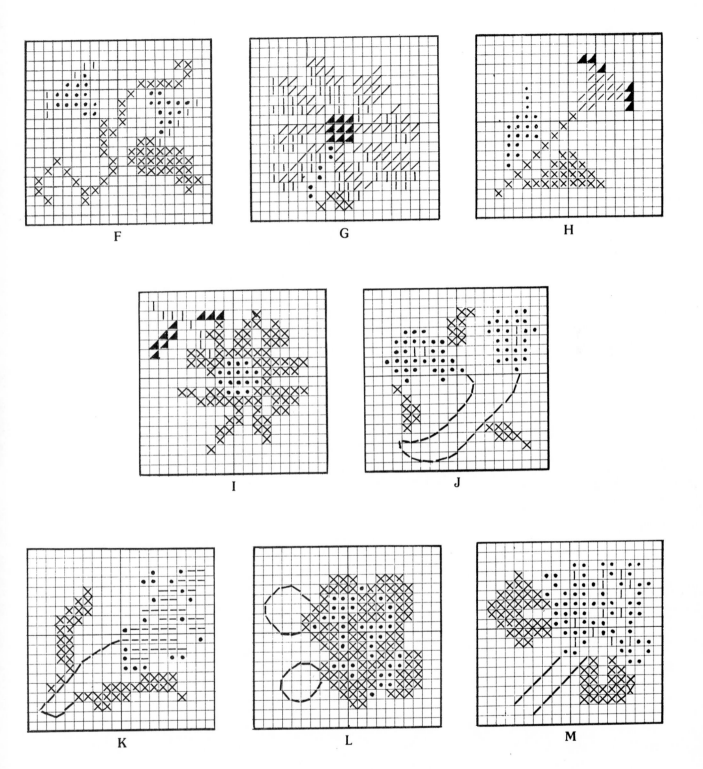

F

G

H

I

J

K

L

M

HEIRLOOM AFGHAN IS LIGHTHEARTED "GRANNY"

This splendid, sweeping afghan is a traditional "granny," but a granny with a new twist. That twist is the two-ply weaving yarn that gives the afghan a bubbly, light-as-air look, emphasized by the off-white color of the connecting strips and tassely fringe that tie the 143 crocheted squares together. Use any colors you like for the squares themselves, improvising different combinations as you go along, and using the colors at random, so no two squares are exactly alike.

MATERIALS NEEDED

Berga/Ullman Filtgarn, two-ply weaving yarn:
Approximately nineteen 330-yard skeins (100 grams) in assorted colors, as desired
10 skeins off-white
Crochet hook, size H

See page 86 for list of crochet abbreviations and stitches.

Afghan shown is 94″ x 110″ plus fringe. It is made of 143 squares, each 8½″ x 8½″. Colors are combined at random, and no two squares are identical. Use colors shown in photograph or select any color range desired.

To make each square, begin at center, using any color, ch 4; sl st in first ch to form ring.

Round 1: Ch 3, 2 dc in ring, (ch 2, 3 dc in ring) 3 times, ch 2, sl st in top of ch 3. End off.

Round 2: Join another color in any ch-2 sp, ch 4, 2 tr in same sp, ch 2, 3 tr in same sp, (ch 2, 3 tr, ch 2, 3 tr in next ch-2 sp) 3 times, ch 2, sl st in top of ch 4. End off.

Round 3: Join another color in any ch-2 corner sp, ch 4, 2 tr in same sp, ch 2, 3 tr in same sp, (ch 2, 3 tr in next sp, ch 2, 3 tr, ch 2, 3 tr in corner sp) 3 times, ch 2, 3 tr in next sp, ch 2, sl st in top of ch 4. End off.

Round 4: Join another color in any ch-2 corner sp, ch 4, 2 tr in same sp, ch 2, 3 tr in same sp, (ch 2, 3 tr in next sp, ch 2, 3 tr in next sp, ch 2, 3 tr, ch 2, 3 tr in corner sp) 3 times, (ch 2, 3 tr in next sp) twice, ch 2, sl st in top of ch 4. End off.

Round 5: Join another color in any corner space, work as for rnd 4, having 1 more group of 3 triple crochet on each side.

Round 6: With white, work as for rnd 4, having 2 more groups of 3 triple crochet on each side.

FINISHING: Weave in yarn ends. Arrange squares in pleasing color arrangement, 11 squares by 13 squares. Sc squares together from wrong side, using white and working through sps between sts and over ch sps. For fringe, cut off-white yarn into 8″ strands. Holding 8 strands together, knot strands in every ch-2 sp around edge.

TABLE ART

THE ART OF TABLE SETTING

"**U**se things you live with and love when you set a table," says Gloria Vanderbilt. To match the delicacy of a frosty organdy cloth appliquéd with garlands of pastel flowers and leaves, she takes an exquisite sculpture of translucent shells from its accustomed place to use as a centerpiece, adds shell-shaped plates and real mother-of-pearl shells to hold bread and butter. Her hand-painted goblets are one-of-a-kind treasures, but you can duplicate the appliquéd top cloth.

The word "appliqué," from the French verb *appliquer*, to put on, is used as an adjective, a noun or a verb to describe a method of applying one fabric to another, the piece of fabric applied or the act of applying. This decorative form of needlework can be done by hand or machine, but the finest examples are slipstitched by hand, with stitches so small they can barely be seen on the right side of the finished work. The delicate organdy top cloth used by Miss Vanderbilt for this table setting was done by this method. It was placed over a full-length round cloth of pale pink chintz to show off the appliqués in a bouquet of pastels. You could, of course, substitute a pale version of any of the colors used for the appliqués that suits your color scheme. Cutting diagrams for the appliqués are included in the directions. Any closely woven, lightweight cotton fabric that comes in all the colors you want to use is suitable for the flower appliqués. To achieve the dimensional effect of the appliqués, each flower is composed of four separate layers of fabric—three shades of one color for the petals plus a contrasting color for the center. Both petals and centers are then embroidered for still more dimension and definition. If you take the time to duplicate all this careful handwork, you'll have a cloth of heirloom quality.

FLORAL APPLIQUÉD ORGANDY TABLECLOTH

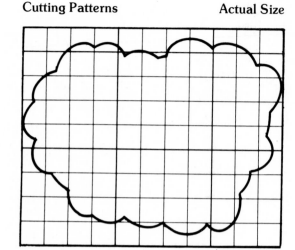

A

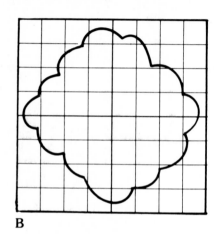

B

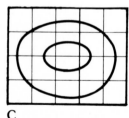

C

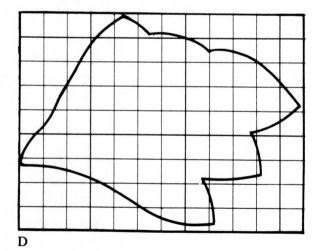

D

MATERIALS NEEDED
(for 54″-square top cloth)

  3 yards white organdy, 44″ wide
  ¼ yard closely woven fabric in each of 14 colors:
  Pale, medium and dark pink
  Pale, medium and dark blue
  Pale, medium and dark yellow
  Pale, medium and dark purple
  Medium and dark green
  Thread to match each color
  Embroidery floss to match dark pink, dark blue, dark yellow, dark purple, medium green and dark green fabrics
  8 yards pale green double-fold bias tape, ¼″ wide

Cut length of organdy in half horizontally. From one 54″ length, cut a 6″-wide strip from each selvedge edge. With right sides together and matching selvedges, stitch one 6″-wide strip to each side of second 54″ length of organdy, stitching just inside selvedges. Using selvedge edges avoids necessity of making French seams; be sure to adjust tension so seams do not pucker. Press seam allowances toward 6″ strips.

From remaining organdy, cut four 11″ x 11″ pieces for napkins.

Appliquéd flowers on cloth are pink, blue, yellow and purple. Each flower is composed of three shades of one color with a contrasting center. Appliquéd flower in one corner of each napkin is a different color.

Trace cutting patterns A, B and C for appliqués. Using Pattern A for medium shade of each color, Pattern B for pale shade and Pattern C for dark shade, cut eleven of each from pink fabric, seven of each from yellow fabric, seven of each from purple fabric and seven of each from blue fabric.

Trace all patterns on wrong side of fabric, adding ⅛" turning allowance around each one.

Trace Pattern D for leaf appliqués. There are 24 medium green leaves and 24 dark green leaves on cloth; pin green fabrics together, right sides facing, and trace leaf appliqué 24 times on wrong side of one. Cut traced appliqués from both fabrics at once, adding ⅛" turning allowance around each one. In addition, cut four D's from dark green fabric for leaves on napkins.

Machine-stitch around each appliqué ⅛" from edge. Turn raw edge to wrong side along stitching line and press, clipping very slightly where necessary.

A circle of appliquéd flowers and leaves in the center of the cloth is surrounded by an eight-pointed star made of two intertwined strips of pale green bias tape worked into scallops (see photograph). Enlarge Diagram 1 on paper ruled in 1" squares to use as pattern for star. Place pattern on right side of cloth so Point 1 is at center of cloth and Point 3 is opposite a corner. Starting at Point 2, trace lightly from Point 2 to Point 4. Holding Points 1 and 4 in place, turn pattern over to trace adjoining point. Turn pattern over twice more in same manner, tracing from Point 2 to Point 4 each time to complete star.

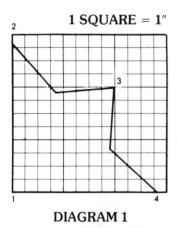

1 SQUARE = 1"

DIAGRAM 1

Single-fold bias tape does not come in ¼" width required for star. To make double-fold tape less bulky and easier to manipulate into scalloped design of star, open folds along both edges of tape and trim raw edges to ⅛". Work first strip of tape into scallops along outline of star, centering them on marked line and folding tape sharply back on itself at points of star (see Diagram 2). Pin tape in place as you work, then baste to cloth and press

with steam. Work second strip of tape into scallops along same outline, crossing over and alternating with first strip of scallops. Curve tape around points of star, covering folded tape underneath. Baste second strip in place and press with steam. Slipstitch tape to cloth along both edges, using matching pale green thread.

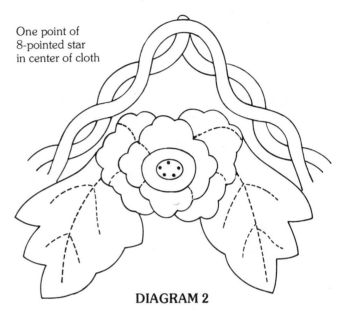

One point of 8-pointed star in center of cloth

DIAGRAM 2

Starting with any of the four flower colors, pin one A and one medium green and one dark green leaf to cloth inside one point of star, following placement shown in Diagram 2. Continue around star, using one A in each of four colors first, then repeating colors in same order. Alternate medium and dark green leaves with each A, so that adjacent leaves are never the same shade of green. Slipstitch each appliqué in place with matching thread.

Complete each flower, placing B on A and C on B as indicated by Diagram 2. Insert a small square of contrasting color beneath each C for center of flower, with raw edges of square covered by C. Slipstitch appliqués in place, using matching thread.

Pin appliqués to edges of cloth on either side of each corner, following placement shown in Diagram 3. Flower at bottom of diagram goes in each corner. Reverse remainder of diagram for adjoining side. Start at each corner with a yellow flower; to one side, use a dark green leaf, then a medium green leaf; on other side, use a medium green leaf, then a dark green leaf. On first side, follow with a

One side of
corner appliqué on cloth

DIAGRAM 3

pink flower, a dark green leaf, a blue flower and a medium green leaf. On other side, follow with a pink flower, a medium green leaf, a purple flower and a dark green leaf. Interchange pink, blue and purple flowers around other corners, but keep order of dark and medium green leaves the same.

Curve short pieces of bias tape around corners of cloth and along edges between appliqués, as indicated by Diagram 3. Measure length of tape needed to connect leaf to flower in each case, then cut, baste in place and press, inserting edges of tape under leaves and flowers.

Slipstitch appliqués and bias tape in place except along edges of cloth, using matching thread. Trim raw edges of cloth even with finished edges of appliqués. Turn remaining, untrimmed edges of cloth under 1/8" and press. Overcast edges of cloth, both with and without appliqués, on all sides, using pale green thread.

Using remaining appliqués, apply a flower and a dark green leaf to one corner of each napkin, adding short strips of bias tape as indicated by Diagram 4. Stitch in place and finish napkin in same manner as cloth.

Corner appliqué on napkin

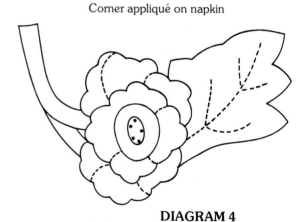

DIAGRAM 4

Remove all basting from cloth and napkins and press. Embroider veins on leaves with outline stitching, following broken lines on diagrams, using contrasting green embroidery floss on each leaf. Embroider petal detail on each flower in same manner, using floss in darkest shade of flower color. Embroider five French knots in center of each flower in contrasting color.

DELICATE WHITE-ON-WHITE TABLECLOTH AND A RUFFLED TEA COZY

When the first spring flowers begin to appear, it's time for a change to lighter, prettier clothing. And that goes for your table. Especially a table that's dressed for a party. Now, one of the prettiest ways you can go to a party is dressed in white. And that goes for your table, too. Certainly one of the freshest-looking cloths your table could wear is this 72"-wide circle of appliquéd and embroidered white organdy. Fine white linen is the thing to use for the appliquéd flowers and leaves and scallopy border—if you can find it. If not, a crisp, white, polished cotton would do very nicely. The great thing about this white-on-white confection (which would cost a not-so-small fortune if you tried to buy it) is that you can use it over another white cloth or over any color. It's pictured here over rosy pink to show off the appliqués and embroidery. Also pictured here, another white-on-white confection: a ruffled tea cozy which also looks delicate and expensive but is a cinch to make. In this case, the embroidery is all done for you, because it's made of eyelet-embroidered batiste, in either a border design or an allover pattern. So all that's involved is some very simple sewing.

APPLIQUÉD CLOTH AND NAPKINS

MATERIALS NEEDED
(for 72″-diameter round cloth and four 17″ x 17″ napkins)

4⅛ yards white organdy, 44″ wide

2¼ yards fine white linen or similar fabric, 44″ wide

Fine white sewing thread

Two skeins white six-strand embroidery floss

Tracing paper

Cut organdy in half across 44″ width. From one piece, cut two lengthwise strips, each 16″ wide. Stitch one 16″-wide strip to each selvedge edge of the 44″-wide piece, making French seams (Diagram 1). To make French seam, place wrong sides of fabric together and stitch ½″ from edges. Carefully trim seam allowances to ¹⁄₁₆″ and press to one side. Turn fabric so right sides are together and press so seam is exactly along edge. Stitch ⅛″ from first seam, enclosing seam allowances. Press

DIAGRAM 1

finished seam allowances away from center. OR, make a zigzag-finished seam: overlap long edges of 16″-wide strips and center piece 1″; stitch through center of overlap and cover stitching with a close, small zigzag stitch. Trim excess fabric close to stitching on both sides.

To cut cloth, fold (but do not crease) organdy in half, matching seams and raw edges; pin the two layers together. Fold in half again, making a square four layers thick; pin the four layers together. To make a string compass for marking circle, tie a knot

at one end of string and pin to center point; stretch string taut, mark 36¼″ from first knot and tie second knot to indicate bottom edge. Working on a flat surface, move string and mark bottom edge by pinning through all four layers of fabric (Diagram 2). Cut through all layers along marked line. Stitch basting lines dividing cloth into halves, quarters and eighths.

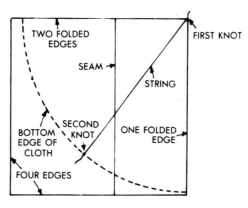

DIAGRAM 2

Diagram 3 is placement guide for one-quarter of cloth; Diagram 4 is placement guide for embroidered quarter of napkins. (Appliquéd border continues around napkin, but only one corner is appliquéd and embroidered with flower motifs.) Broken lines on diagrams indicate dividing lines; heavy lines indicate appliqués; fine lines indicate stem stitch; dotted lines indicate areas filled in with shadow stitch. Tiny circles at centers of flowers are worked in satin stitch. Enlarge both diagrams on paper ruled in 1″ squares. Pin enlarged guide for tablecloth to organdy circle, matching dividing lines. Using light blue dressmakers' tracing paper, transfer all other markings to organdy. Moving enlarged guide around circle, transfer design to all four quarters of cloth.

Enlarge patterns for appliquéd leaves and flowers on paper ruled in ½″ squares and trace onto tracing paper. Using enlarged placement guide for cloth, make a tracing of appliquéd border. Make a tracing of appliquéd border for napkins.

Referring to cutting layout, trace the following number of appliqués on linen (or similar fabric being used): eight border sections for cloth; four A; four B as given and four with pattern reversed; four C; eight D; forty E; twenty-eight F; twenty G. For napkins, trace sixteen border sections; twelve H; eight I; four J. From remaining fabric, cut four

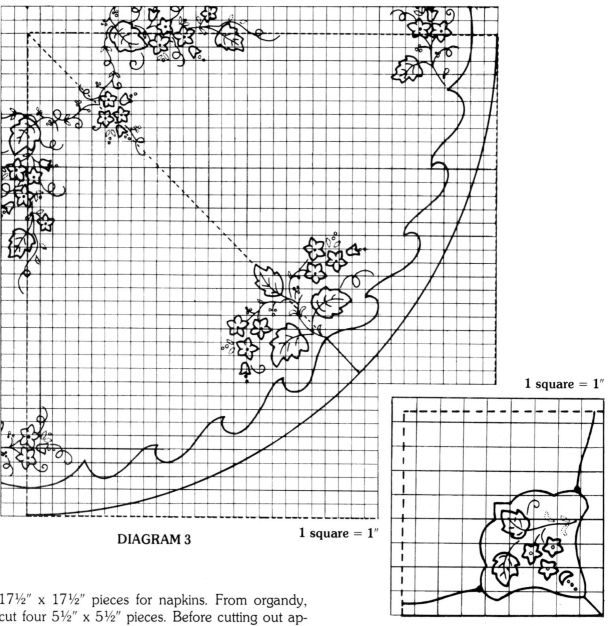

DIAGRAM 3

1 square = 1″

1 square = 1″

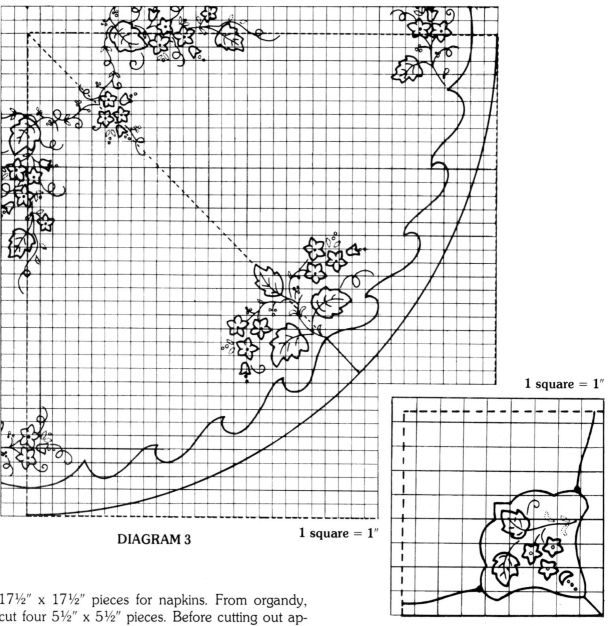

DIAGRAM 4

17½″ x 17½″ pieces for napkins. From organdy, cut four 5½″ x 5½″ pieces. Before cutting out appliqués, machine-stitch along traced outline of each one, then cut ⅛″ beyond outlines of flowers and leaves and top edge of border sections; cut ¼″ beyond side and bottom edges of border sections.

With right sides facing, stitch border sections of tablecloth together ¼″ from side edges, forming a circle. Press seam allowances open. Pin right side of border to wrong side of organdy cloth, matching outlines. Stitch together around edge of cloth, ¼″ from raw edges. Turn border to right side of cloth and press so seam is exactly along edge.

To appliqué border to cloth, clip ⅛″ turning allowance at points and around curves; turn allowance under and finger-press along stitching line.

Baste in place, making sure border lies flat, and appliqué to organdy with either the pin stitch (Diagram 5) or slipstitch (Diagram 6). Since the pin stitch is more intricate and time-consuming, you may prefer to use the easier but equally effective slipstitch. Starting at center of cloth, appliqué each motif in place in same manner as border.

When all appliqués have been applied, proceed with embroidery. Using only two strands of floss in needle, work circles at centers of flowers in satin stitch (Diagram 7). Work all fine lines in stem stitch

(Diagram 8). Fill dotted outlines with shadow stitch (Diagram 9).

To make each napkin, trace design onto one corner of linen square and also onto organdy square, matching edges of placement guide and fabric. Machine-stitch outline of design area and border on napkin. Apply leaf and flower appliqués to organdy square and work embroidery. Leaving ¼" allowance beyond outlines, trim excess organdy away. Cut away design area on napkin, leaving ⅛" allowance inside stitched outline. Clip allowances on both napkin and organdy to circles. Turn ⅛" allowance on napkin to wrong side above circles; appliqué to organdy, matching circles and outlines. On wrong side of napkin, turn edge of organdy under ⅛" and slipstitch to napkin, just catching single threads. Turn ⅛" allowance on napkin to right side below circles and finger-press. Trim organdy to ⅛". Stitch border sections together at corners, taking ¼" seams; press allowances open. Stitch border sections to napkin in same manner as for cloth, with organdy between the two layers of linen at corners, catching all three layers of fabric as you appliqué.

PATTERNS FOR APPLIQUÉS   1 square = ½"

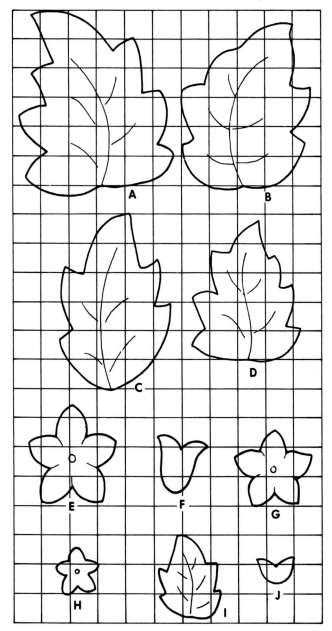

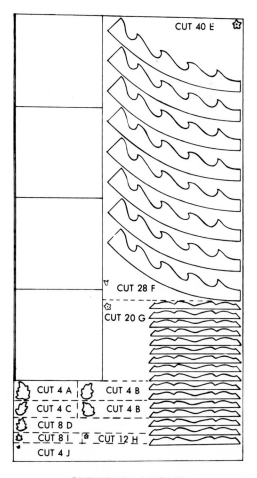

CUTTING LAYOUT

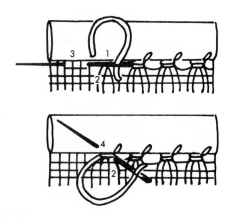

DIAGRAM 5
Pin Stitch

Bring needle through folded edge of fabric at 1, insert at 2 and bring out at 3; insert once more at 2 and bring out at 3. Insert again at 2, bring out through folded edge at 4. Pull all stitches firmly.

DIAGRAM 6
Slipstitch

Working from right to left, bring needle up through fold of appliqué. Directly opposite and barely outside fold, take a stitch, catching only one thread of fabric; then slip the needle through the fold a small stitch length away.

DIAGRAM 7
Satin Stitch

Work straight stitches close together across area to be filled, bringing needle out for each new stitch only a thread beyond previous stitch to achieve solid area of embroidery.

DIAGRAM 8
Stem Stitch

Work from left to right taking regular, slightly slanting stitches along the design line. Always bring up needle at left of previous stitch.

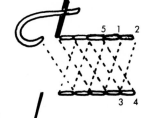

DIAGRAM 9
Shadow Stitch

Work from right side of fabric. Work small backstitches alternately from side to side. Bring needle through fabric at 1, insert at 2, slant needle across wrong side of fabric and bring up at 3, insert at 4, again slant needle across wrong side of fabric and bring up at 5. Fill area in this manner. Dotted lines on diagram show thread on wrong side of the fabric.

TEA COZY

MATERIALS NEEDED
⅜ yard allover eyelet-embroidered fabric
    or
⅞ yard eyelet-bordered fabric
⅞ yard eyelet ruffling, 1¼″ wide
½ yard bleached muslin
Polyester batting

Tea cozy is made of eyelet-bordered fabric, but eyelet-embroidered fabric in an allover pattern would be equally effective.

Enlarge Diagrams 1 and 2 on paper ruled as indicated to use as patterns. From eyelet-embroidered fabric, cut two sections for cover; cut one tab. From muslin, cut two pieces for lining, placing fold line of tea cozy pattern on lengthwise fold of fabric to obtain two large muslin ovals. Transfer all pattern markings to fabrics. Using the same pattern, cut eight pieces of batting for interlining.

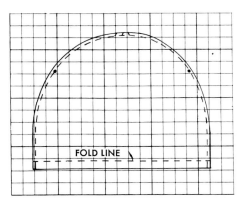

DIAGRAM 1   1 square = 1″

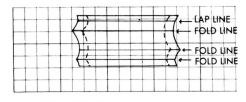

DIAGRAM 2   1 square = ½″

Turn ¼″ to wrong side along straight edge of each section for cover and press, then turn another ⅜″ to wrong side; stitch along first fold. With right sides together, pin straight edge of ruffling along curved edge of one cover section, turning cut ends

of ruffling parallel with seam allowance so raw edges will be caught in seam.

On piece for tab, fold fabric to wrong side along three fold lines, overlapping seam allowance on one side to lap line. Stitch along center fold through all four thicknesses. Fold in half and pin ends to ruffled cover section where indicated on pattern, with one end on top of ruffling and other end underneath it, keeping all edges even. Baste tab and ruffle in place. With right sides facing, pin cover sections together around curved edges, enclosing ruffling and tab. Stitch together ⅜″ from edges and turn right side out.

To make padded lining, stay-stitch both ends of each piece of muslin between circles, ⅜″ from edges. Fold each piece in half, matching curved

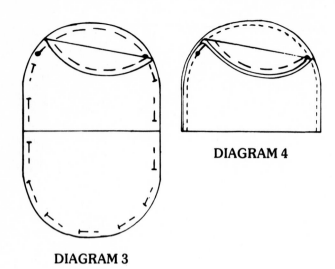

DIAGRAM 4

DIAGRAM 3

ends, and press folded edge. Matching both folded and raw edges all around, place one folded piece on top of the other. Pin together from circles down to fold on each side (Diagram 3). Stitch together ⅜″ from edges. Turn to right side.

Matching edges, stack four pieces of batting on top of each other to pad each side of lining; insert through opening on each side. Turn raw edges of each opening to inside along stay-stitching and finger-press; slipstitch openings closed. Slip cover over lining and tack together if desired, or leave separate so cover can be laundered separately.

SOME OF
GLORIA'S
FAVORITE
THINGS

Gloria's private domain is drenched with dazzling sunlight, sparkling color and a multitude of favorite objects—treasures large and small she has collected from far and near. As might be expected, many of her favorite things are made of, covered with or decorated with fabric—often in her own exuberant designs, but always with her special flair for pattern and color. A standard writing pad, for instance, isn't standard at all because it's covered with exploding bouquets of flowers—and a utilitarian telephone book is camouflaged by feminine checked gingham frosted with embroidered braid and lace. You might enjoy owning and using the same things—and you can.

The writing pad is covered in a colorful, flower-printed cotton, protected by a stain repeller. Her own telephone book cover, left, is in pale violet-and-white checks; you could substitute any pastel (or pattern) you prefer, and select your own trio of decorative trimmings. The small picture frame, opposite, curvaceous and lightly padded, has a faintly Victorian flavor. It's covered in a miniflowered cotton print.

FABRIC-COVERED WRITING PAD

MATERIALS NEEDED
Illustration board, 30″ x 40″
1 yard printed fabric, 36″ wide or wider
One 8½″ x 12″ blotter
¼ yard cotton canvas
Polyester batting
White glue
Mat knife
Masking tape and pins

From illustration board, cut four 9½″ x 13″ pieces, two 8½″ x 12″ pieces, and one 5″ x 12″ piece. Cut two 4″ x 12″ strips of cotton canvas.

With wrong sides facing, glue two pieces of illustration board together for front of writing pad and two pieces together for back of pad. When glue is dry, place boards side by side as shown in Diagram 1, with 1″ space between them. Center one strip of canvas over inner edges of boards, bridging space between them, with boards extending ½″ beyond top and bottom edges of canvas. Glue canvas strip firmly to boards and allow glue to dry.

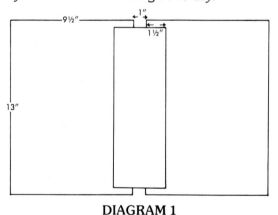

DIAGRAM 1

Cut two 8½″ x 12″ pieces of batting to pad front and back of writing pad. Center one layer of batting on each board and glue corners in place. If thicker padding is desired, tack two layers of batting together at the edges before gluing to each board.

Cut a 17½″ x 24½″ piece of fabric for outside covering so dominant motif of pattern will be centered on front cover of writing pad when fabric is centered over boards. Also cut one 9½″ x 16½″ piece of fabric, one 12½″ x 16″ piece, one 5″ x 13″ piece, and four 4″ x 4″ pieces, with fabric pattern going in same direction on all pieces.

Center fabric for outside covering over padded boards, with pattern in desired position on front cover. Fabric should extend about 2″ beyond boards on all sides. Pin fabric to batting in a few places to keep it in position while you turn boards over. Keeping inner edges of boards 1″ apart, wrap fabric around outer edges, pulling it taut equally from side to side and from top to bottom; tape the 2″ overlap in place temporarily along all edges, mitering fabric at corners as shown in Diagram 2. Check to make sure fabric fits smoothly and pattern is straight on covered sides of boards. Adjust if necessary and glue overlap to inside edges of boards and to canvas. Allow glue to dry.

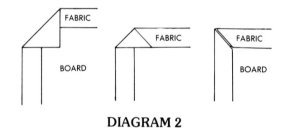

DIAGRAM 2

Center second strip of canvas on wrong side of 5″ x 13″ strip of fabric; pull ½″ margin of fabric around top and bottom edges of canvas and glue overlap to canvas. With writing pad open and fabric side of strip up, center strip over inner edges of boards and glue in place.

To make pocket to hold writing paper on inside of front cover, first cover one 8½″ x 12″ board with 12½″ x 16″ fabric. Center right side of board on wrong side of fabric and pull edges of fabric around edges of board so fabric fits smoothly and pattern is straight. Glue overlap to board, mitering fabric at corners. While glue is drying, pad 5″ x 12″ piece of illustration board with a 4″ x 11″ piece of batting. Center board on wrong side of 9½″ x 16½″ piece of fabric, padded side down. Wrap fabric around one long edge of board only and glue overlap to unpadded side of board.

Place 5″-wide board on 8½″-wide board, both with fabric sides up, and with uncovered edges of narrow board flush with edges of wider board along top, bottom and right side. Holding boards firmly together, turn them both over so uncovered side of 8½"-wide board is on top (Diagram 3). Keeping boards in position, wrap extending fabric around edges of both boards and pull it tautly enough to stretch it smoothly over narrow board. Tape overlap to 8½"-wide board, mitering corners. Check placement of pattern on right side of narrow board and glue overlap in place. With writing pad open, center pocket on inside of front cover, covered side up. Glue in place.

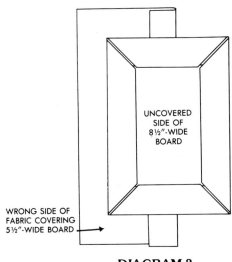

DIAGRAM 3

Blotter on right side of writing pad is backed by remaining 8½" x 12" piece of illustration board and held in place by four triangular pockets of fabric. On illustration board, mark off 2" along both sides of each corner. Draw diagonal line connecting each pair of marks. Fold each 4" x 4" square of fabric in half diagonally to form a triangle and press fold. Center a traingle over each corner or right side of board with fold along diagonal line. Tape triangles to right side of board temporarily and turn board to wrong side. Fold extending fabric around edges of board and glue to wrong side, mitering corners. When glue is dry, center board on right side of writing pad and glue in place. Slip blotter into fabric corners.

TELEPHONE BOOK COVER

MATERIALS NEEDED
  1¼ yards fabric, 36" wide or wider
  1¼ yards interfacing
  ½ yard cotton canvas
  1¼ yards embroidered sheer trim, 1" wide
  1 yard embroidered braid, 1" wide
  1 yard Venice lace, ⅝" wide
  Lightweight, pliable cardboard
  Thread to match background of fabric

NOTE: The standard size of telephone books in the United States is 9" x 11", but the thickness varies. The specifications given here are for a cover which will fit telephone books from 1¾" to 2⅜" thick. For thinner or thicker books, adjust widths of materials according to thickness of spine.

From outer fabric, cut a piece 12½" deep x 38½" wide to wrap from the inside front cover, around outside of book and continue across inside of back cover. Cut a separate piece of fabric 12½" deep x 7½" wide to face the center section that covers the spine of the book. Cut a piece of interfacing 12½" deep x 38½" wide. Cut a piece of canvas 12½" deep x 21½" wide to reinforce outer section of cover. Cut a piece of cardboard 11½" deep x 21½" wide.

Place interfacing on right side of outer fabric with all edges flush; stitch together along short sides only, ½" from raw edges. Trim seams to ¼", turn fabric right side out, and press.

Center canvas on interfacing, with top and bottom edges flush and interfacing extending 8½" beyond canvas on either side; pin canvas to interfacing and fabric (Diagram 1).

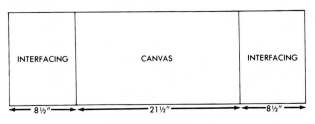

DIAGRAM 1

Turn ¼" to wrong side along each long edge of 7½" x 12½" piece of fabric for spine facing; stitch close to folds. Center facing on fabric side of cover, right sides together and top and bottom edges flush; pin in place along top and bottom edges. Beginning at side edge of spine facing, stitch facing, outer fabric, interfacing, and canvas together ½" from top and bottom edges. Trim seams to ¼" and turn facing to canvas side of cover.

With outer fabric right side up, fold right and left edges of cover toward center along edges of canvas and press. Clip seam allowances at either side of spine facing so that top and bottom raw edges lie flat. Stitch ½" from raw edges across top and bottom of pockets, ending each seam at side edge of facing. Trim seams and remaining unstitched seam allowances to ¼", and turn pockets to inside of cover; press so seams are along edges. Inside edges of pockets should overlap spine facing. Turn remaining raw edges to inside and slipstitch in place.

Place 1"-wide embroidered sheer trim wrong side up around edge of front section of cover, with outside edge of trim exactly along edge of cover on three sides and 9¼" from edge of cover along spine. Pin trim in place temporarily and cut to fit. To make mitered corners, pinch trim together diag-onally at corners so it lies flat on cover and mark seamlines along folds (Diagram 2). Remove trim and stitch along marked lines. Trim excess fabric close to stitching and press seams. Blindstitch trim to cover along outer edge.

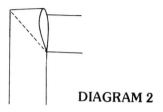

DIAGRAM 2

Place embroidered braid around cover with outer edges of braid just overlapping inner edge of sheer trim. Miter corners in same manner as before and blindstitch braid to sheer trim along one edge and to cover fabric along the other. Place Venice lace around cover next to embroidered braid, with edges just touching; miter corners and tack both edges of lace to cover fabric. Mitered seams of trims should meet at each corner.

Insert precut cardboard in inside pockets of cover and slip finished cover over telephone book, creasing cardboard insert along edges of book's spine.

COVERED PICTURE FRAME

MATERIALS NEEDED

Illustration board, 15″ x 20″
½ yard printed cotton fabric
Polyester batting
Mat knife
White glue
Pins or tape

9″ x 7″ stand-up frame has covered, lightly padded front with 3″ x 4″ oval opening for picture and flat, covered back. Covered easel attached to back supports frame.

Using paper ruled with 1″ squares, enlarge outlines in graph to make patterns and cut out. From illustration board, cut two A's and one C. Cut oval opening indicated by broken line in front A only.

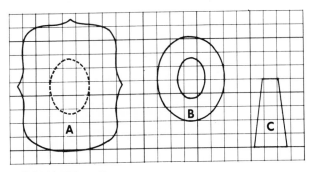

1 SQUARE = 1″

Cut 9½″ x 11½″ piece of fabric to cover front A. Center Pattern B on wrong side of this piece and trace inner edge of oval; cut out along marked oval.

To make facing for covering of front A, trace Pattern B on fabric and cut out. Place facing on covering, right sides together, with inner edges of ovals even. Stitch covering and facing together around inner oval, ½″ from raw edges. Trim close to stitching and clip into seam allowances at 1″ intervals all around oval. Turn facing to inside and press so seam is exactly along edge of oval.

Cut 1¾″ strips of batting and glue in place

around front A, centering them on width of frame. Place covering for front A over padded frame, matching oval openings, and pull facing through oval to back of A. Keeping seam along exact edge of oval, glue facing firmly to back of A.

After glue has dried thoroughly, pull fabric around outer edges of frame, clipping wherever necessary to make fabric fit smoothly over front; pin or tape edges of fabric to back of A. (Excess fabric must be overlapped considerably on back to fit smoothly over front.) Turn frame to right side and fill any puckers with small quantities of batting, giving padding a rounded shape while smoothing and adjusting fabric so covering is not lumpy. When covering fits smoothly, trim execss fabric on back and glue securely in place.

Cut second 9½″ x 11½″ piece of fabric to cover back of frame and center over back A. Pull fabric tightly around edges and pin or tape to back; check covered side to make sure fabric is smooth. Trim excess fabric on back and glue securely in place.

Place Pattern B on fabric and trace around outer edge of oval; cut out oval. Center fabric oval on uncovered side of back A and glue in place, so exposed oval of back A will be covered when front A is placed over it; see photograph.

Place front A over back A, matching edges, and glue firmly together, leaving at least ½″ around oval free of glue to accommodate picture.

Trace Pattern C twice on wrong side of fabric; add ½″ all around outlines for seam allowance and cut out. Stitch together, right sides facing, leaving bottom edges open. Trim seam allowances close to stitching, clip corners, and turn right side out. Slip support C into fabric covering, turn edges of fabric to inside along bottom edge of support, and slipstitch covering closed.

Place support vertically on back of frame, centering it on width, and with top edge midway between top and bottom edges of frame. Slipstitch in place to back of frame.

Cut a ¾″ x 4½″ strip of fabric for tape attachment. Fold strip in half lengthwise, right sides together, and stich close to edges, leaving one end open. Turn right side out, slipstitch opening closed and press. Tack one end of tape to back of frame, 1½″ from center of bottom edge. Tack other end of tape to inside of support, 1½″ from center of bottom edge. Check to make sure that frame stands properly, then slipstitch tape in place.

LACY
COLLAGES
IN
PILLOW
FORM

Wouldn't you know these two beauties belong to Gloria? Decorative pillows spill all over her colorful, eclectic apartment, and these are two of her favorites. Small wonder, when you realize how much they resemble her own lacy, beribboned collages— or the Victorian valentines she loves so much. But these delectable versions are worked on plump, unbleached muslin pillows 18½" square. In the center of each is a square of old patchwork—one an embroidered crazy quilt of satin and velvet, the other more rustic in calico and muslin. Start with a scrap of old patchwork or start from scratch, and add layers of lace edging and ribbons and ruffles.

MATERIALS NEEDED
(for each 18½"-square pillow)

- ⅝ yard unbleached muslin, 44" wide
- ⅝ yard lace, 44" wide
- 2¼ yards crochet lace ruffling, 3½" wide
- Matching thread
- Polyester fiberfill

Also, for Pillow with Crazy-Quilt Center
- Piece of crazy quilt, 7½" square
- 1⅛ yards scalloped lace edging, 2" wide
- 1⅛ yards pale green velvet ribbon, 1¼" wide
- 1¾ yards pale green velvet ribbon, ¾" wide
- 1¾ yards lace beading, 1¼" wide

Also, for Pillow with Patchwork Center
- Piece of geometric patchwork, 8½" square
- 1½ yards crochet lace edging, ⅞" wide
- 1½ yards lace edging with one straight edge, 2" wide
- 2 yards scalloped lace edging, 2" wide
- 3½ yards beige grosgrain ribbon, 1¼" wide

NOTE: Pillows shown are made with natural-to-ecru-color lace, edgings and ruffling, for the currently fashionable "natural" look. White laces could be substituted if desired, with basic pillow cover made of white fabric. Edgings, ruffling and ribbon specified are exactly as shown, but other widths and ribbon colors could be used.

For each pillow, cut two pieces of muslin and one piece of lace, each 19½" square. Place lace on right side of one piece of muslin, matching edges. Smooth lace flat over muslin and stitch together ½" from edges. Center crazy-quilt or patchwork square on lace and stitch in place, ¼" from edges of square. Following diagrams and individual instructions for each pillow, pin ribbon and lace edgings in place, cutting mitered corners. Using zigzag stitch, stitch ribbon and edgings in place, stitching along straight edges or just inside scalloped edges and over diagonal mitered edges.

PILLOW WITH CRAZY-QUILT CENTER

Pin inside edge of 2"-wide lace edging around center square, overlapping patchwork ¼"; place 1¼"-wide velvet ribbon under lace edging and zigzag-stitch both in place at once, stitching inside scallops along both edges of lace. Pin lace beading over ¾"-wide velvet ribbon around outside of top section, 1½" from raw edges; zigzag-stitch lace in place along both edges.

PILLOW WITH PATCHWORK CENTER

Cut strips of narrow crochet lace edging to form diamond pattern within square of patchwork, outlining sections of patchwork if possible (see photo) and stitch in place along outer edges only. Place grosgrain ribbon around square, overlapping patchwork ¼", and place 2"-wide lace edging over grosgrain, with straight edge inside. Stitch both in place at once, along inner edges. Zigzag-stitch over edges of ribbon and then over mitered corners, but leave scalloped edge of lace free. Place 2"-wide scalloped lace edging over grosgrain ribbon ¾" from edges of top section; zigzag-stitch both in place at once, stitching inside scallops along both edges of lace.

To complete either pillow, pin 3½"-wide lace ruffling around finished top section, right sides together and with heading of ruffling flush with raw edges of top section. Join ends of ruffling with a ½" seam where ends meet, trimming away any excess. Stitch ruffling in place. Place muslin bottom section over top section, right sides together, enclosing ruffling. Stitch together ½" from edges, leaving an opening about 8" long along one side. Turn cover to right side and stuff with fiberfill. Turn raw edges in ½" and slipstitch opening closed.

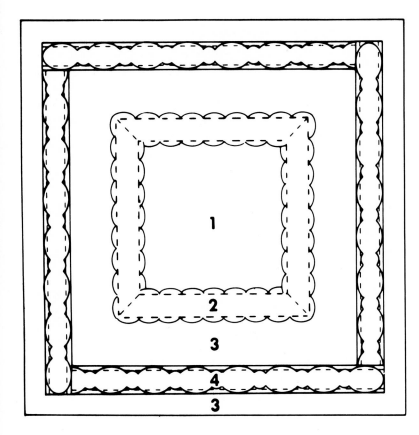

Key to Pillow with Crazy Quilt
1 Square piece of crazy quilt
2 Scalloped lace edging over pale green velvet ribbon
3 Lace over muslin (pillow cover)
4 Lace beading over pale green velvet ribbon

Key to Pillow with Geometric Patchwork
1 Square of geometric patchwork
2 Crochet lace edging
3 Lace edging over beige grosgrain ribbon
4 Lace over muslin (pillow cover)
5 Scalloped lace edging over beige grosgrain

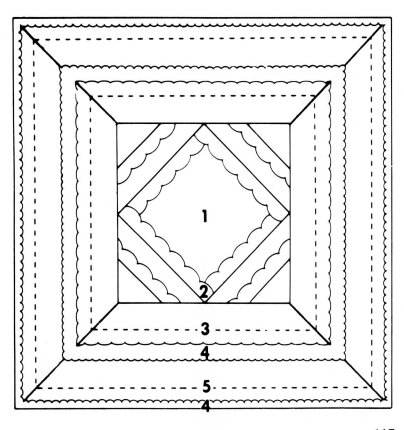

CREWEL PILLOW RECALLS EARLY AMERICAN CRAFTSMANSHIP

One of the earliest of needle arts, crewel embroidery has been practiced for at least a thousand years, and reached a peak of popularity in America early in the eighteenth century, when Colonial ladies first had sufficient leisure to indulge in decorative embroidery. This pillow displays the traditional forms of the popular Tree of Life design—the curvaceous flowers and oversize leaves that have timeless appeal. The embroidery is done in easy chain stitch, then the fabric is padded and quilted by machine to increase the dimensional effect.

MATERIALS NEEDED

- 1¼ yards ecru-color heavy cotton fabric
- 2¼ yards covered cording to match fabric, ¼" diameter
- Matching thread
- Embroidery needle
- 1 layer polyester batting, 20" x 25"
- ¾ yard muslin
- Polyester fiberfill for stuffing
- Tracing paper
- Dressmakers' tracing paper
- Embroidery hoop or frame
- Paternayan Persian yarn:
  - #427 Gold, 18 yards
  - #144 Brown, 16 yards
  - #174 Light Brown, 6 yards
  - #352 Light Blue, 10 yards
  - #330 Blue, 8 yards
  - #137 Lilac, 4 yards
  - #127 Purple, 5 yards
  - #025 Beige, 5 yards
  - #566 Pale Green, 4 yards
  - #532 Green, 9 yards
  - #522 Blue/Green, 10 yards
  - #050 Black, 17 yards
  - #294 Pink, 5 yards
  - #236 Cranberry, 5 yards
  - #184 Grey, 3 yards
  - #975 Pale Orange, 3 yards

Enlarge pattern for embroidery onto paper ruled in 1" squares. From ecru fabric, cut two 20" x 25" rectangles. Using dressmakers' tracing paper, transfer embroidery pattern to one piece of fabric, centering it on the right side of fabric. Tape edge of fabric or turn under and stitch along fold to prevent fraying.

All embroidery is done in chain stitch, using one ply of the three-ply yarn. Use an embroidery hoop or frame to keep fabric taut. Work continuous lines of chain stitch to fill each area, following shape of outline; work circular areas from the center out toward edge in one continuous spiral. Refer to chart and color key for color placement shown in photograph.

After all embroidery is complete, place embroidered piece facedown on a padded surface and press.

To quilt top section of pillow, cut a piece of muslin 20″ x 25″. Place a layer of polyester batting on top of muslin and the embroidered piece (right side up) on top of the batting, with all edges even. Pin all three layers together to keep them from shifting. Stitch around outlines of all embroidered motifs, using either a backstitch or a straight machine stitch and stitching through all three layers. When quilting is complete, remove pins.

To complete pillow: Using zipper foot, stitch cording in place around right side of embroidered piece 1″ from raw edges of fabric, with seam allowance of cording toward edge of fabric. (Cording should butt against edges of embroidery.) To join ends of cording, turn covering of one end back and cut off ½″ of cord; turn raw edge in ¼″, insert other end of cording into fabric covering and stitch ends together. Place embroidered piece on 20″ x 25″ piece of fabric for back of pillow, right sides together, enclosing cording; pin in place. Using zipper foot, stitch top and back sections together along outer edge of cording, leaving a 5″ opening in center of one long edge. Trim seam allowances to ½″. Turn cover right side out and stuff plumply with fiberfill. Slipstitch opening closed.

COLOR CHART FOR CREWEL PILLOW

Color Key

1 Gold, #427
2 Brown, #144
3 Light brown, #174
4 Light blue, #352
5 Blue, #330
6 Lilac, #137

7 Purple, #127
8 Beige, #025
9 Pale green, #566
10 Green, #532
11 Blue-green, #522
12 Black, #050

13 Pink, #294
14 Cranberry, #236
15 Grey, #184
16 Pale orange, #975

CHAIN STITCH
Bring needle up through fabric; hold loop with thumb and insert needle again at same place. Working downward, bring needle up a short distance away with thread looped under needle; repeat. Fill all outlines on chart with rows of chains, following shape of each outline.

BEADED BOUQUETS BRING BACK A TOUCH OF ELEGANCE

Exquisite flowers you can create with transparent and opaque beads have a sparkling freshness that rivals rather than imitates the dew-kissed natural variety. "They're not like 'artificial' flowers at all," says Gloria Vanderbilt of the vibrant blossoms in her large and varied bouquet. "You can bend them and shape them—they have a kind of contained life of their own." You can duplicate the large bouquet that's a shimmering showpiece or make the more modest arrangement that's equally charming, in a smaller way.

GENERAL DIRECTIONS FOR MAKING BEADED FLOWERS

The beaded bouquets are made with size 11/0 round beads, both transparent and opaque, which come on strands of thread, twelve strands to a bunch. You'll need jeweler's pliers and a wire cutter in addition to materials listed for each bouquet. Individual beaded flowers are made by stringing beads onto 28-gauge beading wire, lacing wire or stem wire and shaping wire into petals, stamens, leaves and other flower parts.

Unwind about one yard of 28-gauge wire and wrap it once around thumbtack pushed into one end of spool (to keep remaining wire wound neatly on spool). Carefully pull one strand of beads from bunch; knot thread at one end. At other end of strand, insert end of wire through five or six beads at a time and carefully pull thread out. Continue until designated number of beads have been strung on wire, unwinding more wire from spool as needed; allow at least 12″ of extra wire and rewrap wire around thumbtack. Knot or crimp wire at threading end; do not cut beaded wire from spool. Keep beading close and tight so as little wire as possible shows.

Basic techniques for shaping flowers from wire threaded with the required number of beads are given here. Refer to specific directions for amounts and colors of beads required for individual flowers shown in photographs of bouquets.

BASIC LOOP

The basic loop is used to form petals and leaves and can be made with rounded or pointed ends. Slide designated number of beads from spool onto

wire and to within 3″ of knotted end. At end of beads opposite knot, make a bare wire loop, using about 6″ of wire; twist several times to secure loop (Diagram 1). Slide the same number of beads as in first row up to loop, adding two more if making a rounded end, or four more if making a pointed end. Curve this second row up and around one side of first row and loop wire around bare wire just above beads. For third row, slide up same number of beads as in second row, plus two or four additional beads, depending on whether end is to be rounded or pointed (Diagram 2). Curve this row down on other side of first row and twist wire around original twist. Continue making additional rows, adding two or four beads to each (depending on rounded or pointed end) and curving wire to alternate sides; finish at loop end, which will be stem of flower. Cut wire from spool 4″ from beading; cut knotted end of wire ¼″ from beads and bend end down behind beads. Cut loop open and twist ends together with end of wire cut from spool. Flatten and shape completed leaf or petal.

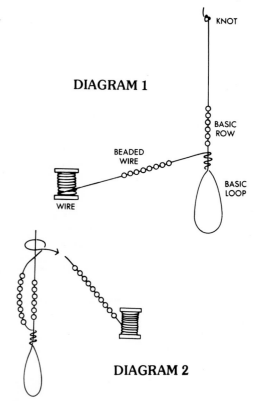

DIAGRAM 1

DIAGRAM 2

SINGLE LOOP

Slide designated number of beads to within 3″ of knotted end of wire; shape beaded wire into loop.

Cross bare ends of wires and twist together twice (Diagram 3). For continuous single loops, continue making loops in same manner, always twisting wires together between each loop. When loop is complete, leave 4" of bare wire and cut from spool.

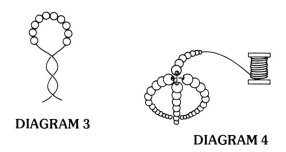

DIAGRAM 3

DIAGRAM 4

CROSSOVER LOOPS

Make single loop of designated number of beads but twist wires only once; then curve beaded loop into a long oval shape. Slide up same number of beads as in single loop; carry half of beads across face of loop, with wire between two top beads of single loop (Diagram 4). Bring remaining half of beads down behind single loop and twist wires twice. Flatten and shape completed petal with your fingers. Continue making crossover loops. When desired number of petals are completed, leave 4" of bare wire and cut from spool.

STRAIGHT STAMENS

For one pair of stamens, thread forty yellow beads onto 28-gauge wire. Coil the end of the wire tightly around a large needle three times; remove needle. Slide twenty beads up to coil and make a 6" loop of bare wire below beads. Slide remaining twenty beads to loop and coil the spool end of wire around the needle three times. Cut wire at both ends close to coils. Cut bottom of loop open and twist cut ends of wire together.

WRAPPING STEM WITH BEADS

String two strands of green beads onto lacing wire. Wrap 1" of bare wire at end without knot around the stem below flower. Slide beads up to flower and wrap beads tightly around stem by twirling flower with one hand while holding beaded wire taut with other hand. (Holding flower upside down may make it easier to wrap beads tightly.) Cover stem with beads to within several inches of bottom end and wrap wire around stem several times; cover exposed wire and stem with tape.

LEAVES

For number of leaves required, see specific directions for individual flowers. To make narrow leaf, thread about 27" of green beads onto wire. Leaf is made in basic loop technique, with a starting row of beads about 5" long. Work five rows, making a pointed top and rounded bottom (at loop end). If you have trouble keeping rows flat and close together, use a bobby pin to hold them in place. When beading is complete, reinforce leaf with lacing across the center: using a short length of lacing, wrap the middle of the wire once around the center row of leaf, halfway between top and bottom. Then, working outward to each side, wrap the lacing wire once around each row, keeping the rows close together; wrap wire twice around each outside row and cut wire close to beads.

To make wide leaf, thread about 77" of green beads onto wire. Leaf is made in basic loop technique, with a starting row of beads about 6" long. Proceed in same manner as for narrow leaf, but make this leaf eleven rows wide. When beading is complete, cut wire at knotted end to 1½" length. Place stem wire down center of underside of leaf, with top of wire and top of leaf even. Wrap top end of wire around stem wire; twist bottom end of wire around stem wire. Lace as for narrow leaf, but begin lacing at stem wire.

ASSEMBLY

If flower has stamen center, arrange petals in a circle around lower edge of stamen. Twist ends of all wires together several times. To make smooth stem, cut off ends of wires at slightly varying points. Cut stem wire of appropriate gauge to desired length. Hold flower wires against stem wire. Tear off about 20" of floral tape and stretch it; then wrap it smoothly around stem wire, working diagonally downward and overlapping edges of tape so wire is completely covered. Attach leaves by wrapping them onto stem so their tips are level with bottom of flower; continue wrapping down the stem. Shape flowers and leaves, arranging them as desired.

LARGE BEADED BOUQUET

MATERIALS NEEDED

Round beads, size 11/0, in these approximate amounts:

    12 bunches opaque white
     1 bunch transparent white opal
    16 bunches opaque royal blue
    12 bunches transparent light blue
     2 bunches opaque yellow
    18 bunches transparent medium green
Stem wires:
        3 packages 16-gauge, 12″ long (42-count)
        3 packages 14-gauge, 12″ long (26-count)
    10 rolls green floral tape
     3 spools silver-colored lacing wire
    15 spools silver-colored beading wire, 28-gauge
        (90 yards per spool)
    Large pedestal vase

Read and follow general directions for beading on page 124.

Pansy Buds: Bouquet has four blue and four white buds. For each, thread wire with 162 beads of desired color. Make a single loop of 8 beads; around the circumference of the first loop, make a second loop of 18 beads; around the second, make a third loop of 28 beads; this is one petal. Twist wires together twice before making a second petal in the same manner; then twist wires twice and make a third petal. Cut wire from spool 4″ from beading. For the calyx, thread 60 green beads on wire; make three continuous single loops of 20 beads each. To assemble, place calyx directly under flower bud and tape together as described in general directions.

Day Lily Buds: Bouquet has six light blue buds. To make each bud, thread wire with two strands of light blue beads. Use basic loop technique, beginning with a row of 35 beads and working five rows. Make two petals; do not cut off top wire. Place the two petals together, with tips even; twist the top wires together and cut off wire. Twist bottom wires together. Make one leaf in same manner, using one strand of green beads. Twist top wire of leaf onto petals near top; twist bottom wire onto bottom of petals. Twist all together to make tight bud.

Daisy: Bouquet has twelve white daisies. Each daisy has three connected petals for top layer and six connected petals for bottom layer. Each petal is made of crossover loops, using 20 beads for each row, or 40 beads for each loop, so thread on 240 opaque white beads for top layer; thread on 480 white beads for bottom layer. To make one stamen for each daisy, thread 44 yellow beads on wire. Make a single loop of 8 yellow beads, twist wire once, then slide 14 beads up to twist. Make a 6″ bare wire loop. Then slide 14 beads up and make another single loop of the remaining 8 beads. Cut wires off close to both bead loops; cut large loop open. For calyx, thread 100 green beads on wire and make five continuous loops of 20 beads each. To assemble, place top layer of petals around stamen, then place bottom layer of petals underneath top layer and calyx underneath petals; twist wires together and tape as described in general directions. Make a narrow leaf and tape onto stem.

Wild Pansy: Bouquet has six white and eight blue pansies. Each flower is made of five petals. To begin, thread wire with about 1 yard of beads in desired color. Make a single loop of 8 beads. Wrap three more single loops, each one larger than the previous one, around the circumference of the original loop; fasten each row by wrapping beading wire around the wire at the base of the original loop each time you encircle it. This completes one petal of four circles. Leave ¼″ of bare wire, then form second petal as you did the first. Continue making petals until you have five in all. For stamen, thread 60 yellow beads on wire. Make five continuous single loops of 12 beads each. For calyx, thread 90 green beads onto wire; make five continuous single loops of 18 beads each. To assemble, encircle the stamen cluster with the petals; just below the petals, attach the calyx. Tape as previously directed, adding a small leaf onto each flower stem. After each flower is taped, tape pairs of flowers and one bud together until you have used all buds; tape remaining pairs of flowers together.

Bluets: Bouquet has eighteen royal blue bluets, each made in three separate parts; each part requires about six strands of beads. For Part I, make eight continuous single loops, using 1″ of beads for each loop. Cut from wire, twist wires together, bend into narrow loops and give each a half-twist. For Part II, make twelve continuous single loops, using 1½″ of beads for each loop. Cut from wire but do not twist wires together. Carefully form narrow loops and give each a half-twist. For Part III, see Diagram 1. Crimp the spool end of wire and slide 1″ of beads to it. Measure 3″ from the crimped end and make three continuous single loops, each formed from 1″ of beads. Slide the original 1″ of beads to the first loop; slide another 1″ of beads from spool to third loop; bring these together and wrap bare spool wire around the end of wire at end of beads. Bring beaded spool wire up along the left side of both 1″ rows, then push bare wire between third and second loops and cross the wire underneath the third loop to the left (Diagram 1). Make two more continuous single loops, each with 1″ of beads; bring 1″ of beaded wire along the left side of the three beaded rows; cut from spool and twist wires together. Make six in all for each flower.

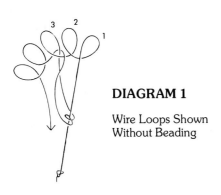

DIAGRAM 1

Wire Loops Shown
Without Beading

For calyx, make five continuous single loops, each formed from 1″ of green beads. To assemble, wrap Part II around Part I and twist wires together. Tape to the top of a taped piece of stem wire. Wrap a piece of lacing wire just below flower to secure flower wires to stem wire. Add the six petals of Part III one at a time, wrapping tightly with lacing wire after adding each one. Wrap lacing wire down another inch, then cut; cut off excess petal wire. Add calyx at base of flower and tape as directed before. Bead the upper stem as directed; make and add a narrow leaf, placing it so its tip is even with lower edge of flower.

Tulip: The bouquet includes fifteen white tulips. Each tulip is composed of five petals. To make each petal, thread one strand of white beads onto wire. Using the basic loop technique, begin with a starting row of 30 beads. Make each petal of eleven rows, forming a pointed top and rounded

bottom. When five petals are completed, tape together onto stem wire. Lace the petals together on inside of each tulip by wrapping lacing wire around two outer rows on each side of each petal, carrying the wire across petal from edge to edge. At beginning and end of lacing, wrap wire twice around beaded petal wire; cut lacing wire close to beading. Bead the upper stem as instructed in general directions. Make and add two long narrow leaves, placing them so their tips are even with the lower edge of the flower.

Day Lily: Bouquet has sixteen day lilies, each with light blue petals changing to royal blue at the center. Each lily has six petals made in the basic loop technique with both ends pointed. In order to shade each petal from royal blue at the bottom to light blue at the top, thread beads on wire in following order: row 7, 24 royal, 22 light blue; row 6, 21 light blue, 22 royal; row 5, 21 royal, 18 light blue; row 4, 18 light blue, 19 royal; row 3, 17 royal, 15 light blue; row 2, 15 light blue, 14 royal; row 1, 14 royal, 12 light blue. Make the basic loop petal, working the seven rows in exact reverse of order given, beginning with the 12 light blue beads of row 1. Make six petals for each flower.

For stamen, make six straight stamens (three pairs), following general directions on page 125. To make the center stamen, thread about 5″ of yellow beads onto wire. Slide 1½″ of beads up, then make three continuous single loops of 12 beads each. Slide another 1½″ of beads up to loops. Cut wire and twist ends together; give 1½″ beaded lengths several half-twists.

To assemble, place looped stamen in center of straight stamens on a short stem. Place six petals around stamen and tape together. Tape pairs of flowers together. Make three narrow leaves and add to each grouping.

Rose of Sharon: Bouquet has twenty-four roses, each consisting of three light blue petals and three variegated petals. For each light blue petal, begin with basic row of 14 beads. Use the basic loop technique to make petal of eleven rows with rounded top and pointed bottom. For each variegated petal, thread on beads in this order: row 11, 13 opal, 9 royal, 21 light blue; row 10, 22 light blue, 10 royal, 11 opal; row 9, 11 opal, 10 royal, 17 light blue; row 8, 18 light blue, 8 royal, 11 opal; row 7, 9 opal, 8 royal, 14 light blue; row 6, 15 light blue, 6 royal, 9 opal; row 5, 25 light blue; row 4,

22 light blue; row 3, 19 light blue; row 2, 17 light blue; row 1, 14 light blue. Make variegated petals in same manner as light blue petals, working the rows in exact reverse of order given, beginning with row 1.

For stamen, make three straight stamens of yellow beads. For looped stamen, make one single loop of 2½" of yellow beads; give several half-twists. Arrange straight stamens around looped stamen. Arrange petals around stamen, alternating solid and variegated petals. Tape stem. Make and add a narrow leaf.

SMALL BEADED BOUQUET

MATERIALS NEEDED
Round beads, size 11/0, in these approximate amounts:
  5 bunches opaque white
  1 bunch opaque alabaster
  3 bunches royal blue
  3 bunches transparent light blue
  8 bunches transparent medium green
Stem wires:
  1 package 16-gauge, 12" long (42-count)
  1 package 14-gauge, 12" long (26-count)
3 rolls green floral tape
5 spools silver-colored beading wire, 28-gauge
1 spool 26-gauge wire (for morning glories)
Small ceramic vase

Read and follow general directions for beading on pages 124–25.

Bluet: Small bouquet has five royal blue and eleven white bluets. Follow directions given for bluets in large bouquet.

Pansy: Bouquet has eight pansies, each predominantly white with alabaster center. Each pansy has five petals made in the basic loop technique, with rounded tops and pointed bottoms. For each petal, thread on beads in following order: row 9, 6 alabaster, 19 white; row 8, 18 white, 5 alabaster; row 7, 5 alabaster, 15 white; row 6, 14 white, 3 alabaster; row 5, 4 alabaster, 10 white; row 4, 12 white; row 3, 8 white; row 2, 6 white; row 1, 3 white. Make basic loop petal, working the nine rows in exact reverse of order given, beginning with row 1.

For the yellow stamen of each pansy, use the basic loop technique, with a basic row of three beads and a second and third row of five beads each. For each leaf, thread about one and a half strands of green beads onto wire. Use the Basic Loop technique, with a basic row of eight beads, to make the leaf thirteen rows wide, with pointed top and rounded bottom. Make three leaves for each pansy.

To assemble, space the five petals evenly around the stamen; tape as directed previously. Tape the three leaves together on a stem; arrange leaves next to pansy in vase.

Morning Glory: Bouquet has twelve light blue morning glories, which are made by a technique not previously described. Cut six pieces of 26-gauge wire, each 4" long; stack together with bottom ends even. Twist wires together very tightly at the bottom, for ¾". (Using two pairs of pliers facilitates tight twisting.) Open out untwisted portions of wires to resemble umbrella spokes; bend wires outward until perpendicular to twisted portion, keeping spokes straight and spaced evenly apart. Thread about three strands of beads onto beading wire; attach cut end of wire by wrapping it two or three times around twisted wires at base of spokes. Near the center, wrap bare wire once around one spoke, going over the top of the spoke and around it. Slide 4 beads up to first spoke; wrap bare wire around second spoke, going over the top of the spoke and around it (see Diagram 2). Slide 4

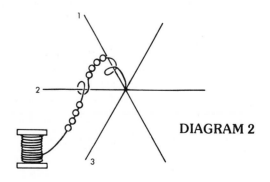

DIAGRAM 2

beads up to second spoke; wrap bare wire around third spoke in same manner as for other spokes. Continue beading between spokes and wrapping wire around spokes, always going over the top of the spoke. Keep spokes as straight and as evenly spaced as possible. Keep beading close together and close to the spokes. For second round, slide 5 beads up between each pair of spokes; continue beading in the same manner as for the first round. For third round, slide 6 beads between pairs of spokes. After the third round, it is not necessary to count beads between spokes; slide up whatever number is necessary to fill spaces between spokes. Work ten rounds in same manner. When beading is complete, wrap bare wire around last spoke, then bring wire down the spoke and wrap around the twisted wire base; cut wire from spool. Cut all but ¼" of wire from end of each spoke; bend each end to underside of flower. Shape flower by bending each section of beading inward.

For stamen, make four continuous single loops of 12 royal blue beads each. To assemble, insert wire ends of stamen through center of flower and twist stamen wires onto twisted flower wires. Tape flower onto an uncut stem wire as described in general directions. Bead the stem as directed before, making it longer than needed, and wrap it around a pencil to coil it.

BASKETS
ARE AN
ART FORM,
TOO

BRIGHTEN
THE LIFE
OF A
BASKET

A market basket from the Philippines, above, gets dressed up for spring in colorful ribbons and rickrack. Any basket woven with wide-open spaces can be given the same pretty treatment; it's a simple matter to weave the ribbons in and out, skipping holes at random or following the basket's own pattern.

You can give any basket a colorful cover—and an organized interior—with a little imagination and a half yard or so of fabric. (Wouldn't it be fun to use a bright flower print to match a favorite summer dress?) Any rectangular basket can be lined like those here—with or without elasticized pockets for sewing paraphernalia.

COVER AND LINING FOR BASKETS

MATERIALS NEEDED
  Printed fabric
  Contrasting lining fabric
  Iron-on interfacing
  Polyester batting
  Elastic, ¼″ wide
  Cable cord, ⅛″ diameter
  Cardboard, light- and medium-weight
  White glue
  T pins

Only rectangular or square baskets with right-angle corners can be lined satisfactorily by the following method. Baskets with rounded sides and ends cannot be lined in this manner.

To make pattern for lining, take inside measurements of baskets as follows, referring to Diagram 1.

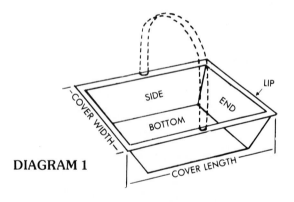

DIAGRAM 1

Measure length and width of bottom or "floor" of basket; draw outline on lightweight cardboard. Measure depth of sides and ends from just under lip at top of basket to floor; measure width across top below lip, and again across bottom at "floor" line; draw outlines on cardboard and cut patterns.

To cut fabric for pockets, measure width of pattern for ends about 1¼″ below top edge; measure depth from that point to bottom edge of pattern. Cut two pieces of printed fabric 1¾ times width and 1½″ deeper than measured depth.

To make pattern for cover, measure width and length across top of basket, measuring from and to outer edges of lip; draw outline on cardboard and mark placement of handle. Determine thickness of handle where joined to basket and draw a semicircular or semioval indentation on each side of pattern wide enough to fit easily around handle. Cut out pattern and mark a circle at each end of indentations.

When cutting printed outer fabric and lining fabric, add ½″ seam allowances on all sides of pattern. Cut one bottom section, two side sections and two end sections from medium-weight cardboard, from printed fabric and from batting. Cut one cover from printed fabric, from lining fabric, from interfacing and from batting.

To cut fabric for pleated edging around cover, measure around outside edge of pattern, excluding indentations for handle; multiply measurement by 1¾ and cut a 2½″-wide strip of printed fabric to length of total measurement.

Top edge of each lining section and edge of cover are finished with narrow cording covered in lining fabric. To determine total length required, measure side and end sections across top edges, adding 1″ to each measurement; add measurement around outside edge of cover pattern plus ½″. Cut enough 1¾″-wide bias strips of lining fabric to equal total measurement. With right sides facing, stitch ends of bias strips together on lengthwise grain, forming one long strip. Fold strip in half lengthwise and place cable cord in fold; using zipper foot on machine, stitch close to cord. Cut pieces of covered cording to length required for each section plus 1″.

Ties for cover are made of bias strips like covered cording, but with the cord removed so ties will be flexible enough to be tied in bows. Cut a 36″ length of cord and cover with bias strip of lining fabric, folding strip around cord with *right* sides of fabric together. Cut covered cord into four 9″ lengths. Stitch across one end of each 9″ strip, stitching through cording. Trim seam allowances at this end to ⅛″ for a distance of about 1″. Holding cord at other end with one hand, gently roll bias covering back on itself and off cord, until entire strip of covering is turned right side out with seam allowances inside. Cut cord away and tie knot in opposite end of bias strip.

To make cover, iron interfacing to wrong side of printed fabric. Measure around edge of pattern, cut a piece of cord to that measurement plus ½″ at each end, and cover with a bias strip of lining fabric. Open stitching slightly at each end; with right sides facing, stitch ends of covering together. Trim cord so ends just meet. Pin covered cording around right side of printed fabric, with raw edges of fabric and cording even. Pin unknotted ends of two ties to right side of fabric at center of each indentation. Stitch cording in place.

To apply pleated edging to cover, cut 2½"-wide strip of printed fabric into two equal lengths. Fold each in half lengthwise, wrong sides together, and stitch ½" from long edges. Pleat each strip, making 1" pleats with ¼" returns; press pleats in place (Diagram 2). Pin pleated strips around right side of lin-

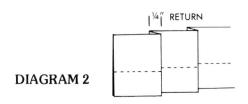

DIAGRAM 2

ing for cover between circles, with raw edges of strip and lining flush, and with ¼" of strip extending at each end; round corners slightly as you stitch, easing in pleats. Cut off any excess pleating beyond the ¼" allowances where indentations begin; turn raw edges at ends of pleating to inside of pleated strip and press. Stitch pleated strips to lining ½" from raw edges.

With right sides facing and raw edges even, pin printed cover and lining together, enclosing pleats and ties. Stitch together close to cording, just inside ½" allowance, leaving an opening for turning at center of one end. Turn to right side and press. Insert batting and slipstitch opening closed.

To apply covered cording to lining sections of basket, pin cording to right side of fabric along top edge of each section, with raw edges of fabric and cording flush. Stitch together ½" from raw edges. Turn allowances to wrong side, leaving only covered cording showing on right side, and press allowances flat.

To apply pockets, run a row of gathering stitches along one long edge of each pocket section. Turn ¼" to wrong side along other long edge and press, then turn another ¾" and press. Stitch in place along first fold, then stitch again 5/16" from first row of stitching to form a casing. Cut a piece of elastic to same measurement as width of end section 1¼" below top edge. Insert elastic in casing and stitch across seam allowance at both ends to secure elastic. With side and bottom edges even, pin wrong side of pocket to right side of end section along side edges. Pull up gathering stitches along bottom edge of pocket to fit bottom edge of end section and pin edges together. Stitch together along side and bottom edges, ½" from raw edges.

Place a layer of batting and then a matching piece of cardboard on wrong side of each side and end section of printed fabric with ½" of fabric extending along side and bottom edges, sliding top edges of batting and cardboard under seam allowances of cording. Apply glue along all edges of cardboard for end sections, but only to top and bottom edges of cardboard for side sections. Fold extending ½" edges of fabric around cardboard and press firmly in place on back.

Apply a few dabs of glue around edge of batting for bottom section; center it on wrong side of printed fabric. Apply glue to a few spots along extending edges of fabric. Apply glue to one side of cardboard for bottom section and press cardboard in place on batting. Place bottom section in bottom of basket, right side up, with edges of fabric extending upward. Apply glue to wrong side of side sections along seam allowance of cording across top edge and to fabric overlap along bottom edge; place in basket and press into position, gluing top edge to basket and bottom edge to extending edges of bottom section.

Apply glue to wrong side of end sections along all edges. Place in basket with side edges overlapping extending edges of side sections. Press in place, gluing top edges to basket and other edges to fabric. Secure all edges with large T pins until glue is thoroughly dry.

PAINT
A BASKET
WITH POSIES

Oh, yes you can! You don't have to be a Picasso to paint a wicker basket. This colorful cache pot and flowering swan don't pretend to be works of art. But they're lots of fun to paint and even more fun to have around after they're finished. First, spray your basket with flat white latex paint. Then, using acrylic paints (or fluorescent poster paints for really high-key colors), paint fantasy flowers on freehand. Still afraid to take the plunge? Using a fabric pattern you like as a guide, just simplify the flowers and place them to suit your basket. Finish by spraying with clear, high-gloss polyurethane. You see? It's easier than you thought.

CROCHET
A
NATURAL
JUTE
BASKET

That's what we said—crochet a basket! Now, isn't that an intriguing idea? If you can do the simplest kind of crochet, you can turn out any one (or all three) of these handsomely textured jute baskets in no time. In fact, even if you've only a nodding acquaintance with a crochet hook, it won't take very long. Because all three are made in much the same manner, with only a few basic stitches. All are made with natural jute cord you can buy in any craft shop. And (naturally) you know that the natural look is the biggest thing going in decorating and all kinds of accessories. You can see how great shells, for instance—or field flowers—look against the natural tawny tones of the rugged jute fiber. The jute cord costs only pennies a yard, so this interesting project will hardly put a hook in your budget.

BASKET WITH DAISIES

MATERIALS NEEDED
(for 5½" basket)
    17 yards ¼" jute cord
    Jiffy crochet hook, size Q
    Small crochet hook

See crochet abbreviations on page 86.

Round 1: Make slip knot, ch 2. Work 8 sc in second ch from hook, sl st in top of ch-2 to join. Pull tail end of cord tight and fasten off.

Round 2: Ch 1, sc in same sp as ch-1. * 2 sc in next sc, repeat from * all around; join (15 sc).

Rounds 3 and 4: Ch 1, sc in same sp. Work 1 sc in each sc; join (15 sc).

Round 5 (handle): Ch 15 tightly (this gives handle its stiffness). Remove hook from lp. Insert hook from outside to inside of basket through top edge opposite start of handle. Insert hook in lp and pull through to outside of basket. Work 1 rnd sl st tightly around edge; do not join.

Round 6: Working in opposite direction from previous rnd, on inside of basket, sl st in each st around. When handle is reached, pull cord behind handle and continue working around. Pull end of cord to inside and fasten off by splitting cord in two and knotting it around a st in the work. Using smaller hook, weave ends neatly into inside of basket.

BASKET WITH SHELLS

MATERIALS NEEDED
(for 8½" basket)
    45 yards ¼" jute cord
    Jiffy crochet hook, size Q
    Small crochet hook

See crochet abbreviations on page 86.

Round 1 (bottom): Make slip knot, ch 2. Work 8 sc in second ch from hook, sl st in top of ch-2 to join.

Round 2: Ch 1, sc in same sp as ch-1. Pull tail end of cord tight and fasten off. * 2 sc in next sc, repeat from * all around; sl st in ch-1 to join (15 sc).

Round 3: Ch 1, sc in same sp. * 2 sc in next sc, sc in next sc, repeat from * all around; join (22 sc).

Round 4: Ch 1, sc in same sp. * 2 sc in next sc, 1 sc in each of next 2 sc; join (29 sc).

Round 5 (braided base edging): Sl st in each sc around; sl st in top thread only of first sl st to join (28 sl st).

Round 6: Ch 1, sc all around; join (28 sc).

Rounds 7 and 8: Ch 1, sc in same sp, sc all around; join.

Round 9: Working tightly in order to pull top edge inward, repeat rnd 8; join. Cut cord and fasten off by splitting cord in two and knotting it around a st in the work. Using smaller hook, weave ends neatly into inside of basket.

BASKET WITH CORAL

MATERIALS NEEDED
(for 7" basket)
    32 yards ¼" jute cord
    Jiffy crochet hook, size Q
    Small crochet hook

See crochet abbreviations on page 86.

Round 1: Make slip knot, ch 2. Work 8 sc in second ch from hook, sl st in top of ch-2 to join. Pull tail end of cord tight and fasten off.

Round 2: Ch 1, sc in same sp as ch-1. * 2 sc in next sc, repeat from * all around; join (15 sc).

Round 3: Ch 1, sc in same sp, * 2 sc in next sc, sc in next sc, repeat from * around; join (22 sc).

Rounds 4, 5 and 6: Ch 1, sc in same sp, sc in each sc around; join (22 sc).

Round 7 (handle): Ch 12; remove hook from lp. Insert hook from outside to inside of basket through top edge opposite start of handle. Insert hook in lp and pull through to outside of basket. Working back along handle, sl st through 1 strand only of each ch until start of handle.

Round 8: Sl st in each sc all around top edge of basket; join and fasten off by splitting cord in two and knotting it around a st in the work. Using a smaller hook, weave ends neatly into inside of basket.

TREASURES
FROM
THE SEA

SHELL-COVERED MIRROR

A *unique treasure created with jewels from the sea. The dramatic winged mirror is simply a piece of plywood cut to fit around an 8"-diameter mirror and paved with curving rows of opaque white shells. Here, it reflects a butterfly poised for flight; look into it yourself and you'll see an angel! The* Natica mamilla *shells and a catalog showing a dazzling variety of other available shells can be ordered by mail. See page 223 for shopping information.*

MATERIALS NEEDED
 12" x 28" plywood, ½" thick
 Clear, fast-drying glue
 Natica mamilla shells in small, medium and large
  sizes
 Round mirror with beveled edge, 8"–8½"
  diameter
 Medium sandpaper
 Flat white paint
 2 small screw eyes
 Picture wire

NOTE: *Natica mamilla* shells in the required quantities of small, medium and large sizes for this project, plus glue, can be purchased in a package for considerably less than they would cost if bought separately. See page 223.

Enlarge diagram on paper ruled in 1" squares to make one-half pattern; complete pattern, cut out and trace on plywood. Using a jigsaw, cut out winged shape. Sand back and edges only; do not sand side to which mirror and shells will be applied. Paint front, back and all edges of the plywood white. When paint is thoroughly dry, center the mirror on plywood and glue in place; circular center section of plywood will extend ¼" to ½" beyond mirror all around. To protect mirror while applying shells, cut a circle of paper slightly smaller than mirror and tape in place temporarily.

Sort shells into two equal groups of small, medium and large sizes. Read through directions and plan placement of shells to use different sizes to

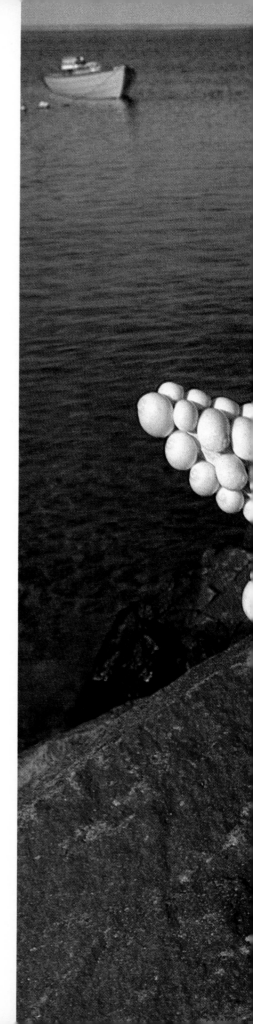

best advantage, with matching shells on two sides of mirror.

Glue a row of small shells to plywood all around mirror, with spiraled ends pointing toward mirror. Working on one wing at a time, place (but do not glue) a row of large shells along top of wing from mirror to tip, using smaller shells at tip if necessary to fit plywood. Keeping the shells in sequence as placed, remove, apply glue and replace each shell in order. As a guide for following rows, draw a few curved lines on plywood, following slightly curved contour of wing. Continue applying curved rows of shells in same manner as first row until wing is covered. Repeat on other wing, using shells in matching sizes.

Beginning at bottom of one wing, apply large shells to ½"-thick lower edge of plywood, covering lower edge of both wings and circle. Beginning at point where one wing meets circle, at top of mirror, glue medium shells to edge of plywood around inside curve, graduating to larger shells across top and decreasing size of shells toward tip. Repeat on other wing, then glue medium to large shells to top edge of circle in same manner. To cover side edges of wings, start with smallest shells in indentations and increase size of shells as you work toward tips. Front surface and all edges of plywood should now be covered. If there are any open spaces, fill in with shells of appropriate size. Remove paper from mirror and allow glue to dry overnight.

Attach two small screw eyes and picture wire to back of mirror and hang.

HALF-PATTERN FOR SHELL-COVERED MIRROR

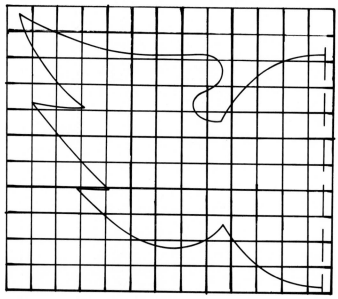

1 Square = 1″

Reverse Pattern for Right-Hand Half of Mirror

SHELL-SHEATHED SWAN

MATERIALS NEEDED
 10"-long wicker swan
 Clear, fast-drying glue
 Absorbent cotton or fiberfill
 2 pounds large pearled umbonium shells
 ½ pound medium-size Venetian pearl shells

Gloria Vanderbilt's beautiful shell-sheathed swan inspired a search for a similar wicker bird which could be covered with the same pearly shells. Alas, the only swan to be found of similar size was more like an ugly duckling than the graceful original. But as we began to glue on the glowing, iridescent shells that sparkle like jewels—lo and behold—the ugly duckling turned into the fabulous swan in the foreground!

NOTE: Shells and glue required for this project can be purchased as a package for considerably less than they would cost if bought individually. See page 223.

Clean shells by washing in warm soapy water, using a soft brush. Rinse in clear water and place on paper towels or newspapers to dry. Sort each variety of shells into groups of matching size.

Choose sixteen or seventeen pairs of matching umbonium shells to go around opening at top of swan. Working with one pair at a time, dab a spot of glue at center of underside of each shell and cover with a small amount of cotton or fiberfill and apply more glue. Place undersides of the two shells together, with shell for outside of swan pointing in one direction and other shell pointing in opposite direction, so they fit together at the top. Holding them in this manner, place the first pair over top rim of swan just behind the neck (see photograph). Hold in place until the two shells stick firmly together and to the wicker on inside and outside of swan. Continue in same manner until top edge of swan is covered with matching pairs of shells. When top row is complete, glue a row of single shells just below it, following the same curve and turning shells in the opposite direction so they fit as closely as possible against shells in top row. Extend second row one shell farther toward front of swan on each side.

Glue on two more rows of the large umbonium shells, covering convex part of swan's body. Glue a row of large umboniums around top of base, with sharp edges of shells fitting into indentation between body and base of swan. Then fill in underpart of body and lower part of base with the smaller Venetian pearl shells. It is not necessary to use cotton or fiberfill to help the smaller shells adhere. Then cover front of swan, neck and head with Venetian pearl shells, using the largest sizes across the front and graduating to smaller sizes as you work up the neck to the head. We filled in the curve where the back of the neck meets the body by gluing a second layer of shells on top of the first one. Finally, fill in any small holes between the large umbonium shells with the smallest Venetian pearls.

TREASURES FROM THE SEA REPRODUCED IN NEEDLEPOINT

Works of art themselves, the exquisite shapes and colors of seashells are a source of inspiration for other artworks. The three striking needlepoint "paintings" seen here are definitely in that category. Sometimes subtle, sometimes bold, the shading of the shells makes them stand out like bas-relief from contrasting backgrounds striped in unexpected colors. They're worked on 12-mesh-to-the-inch canvas in mat-finished cotton and embroidery floss for tridimensional texture.

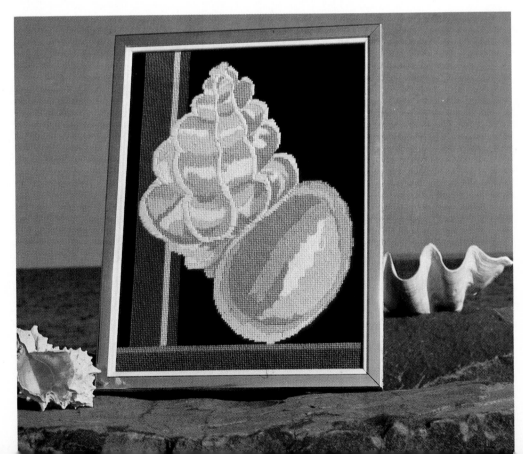

MATERIALS NEEDED

(for each 10" x 13⅝16" picture)

    14" x 17⅝16" mono needlepoint canvas, 12-mesh-to-the-inch

    D.M.C six-strand embroidery floss, used double

    D.M.C mat finished cotton

    Blunt end tapestry needle

    Masking tape

Colors and amounts of embroidery floss and cotton required are listed with color key for each picture. Read general directions for working needlepoint on page 48 before beginning project. Each picture is worked in a combination of two or three stitches: gobelin stitch and brick stitch illustrated on page 153, and continental stitch shown on page 49. Colors used are indicated on each needlepoint chart by symbols within design areas and numbers in background areas. Mark 10" x 13⅝16" outline of finished work on canvas for each picture.

Pink Wentletrap Shell: Outlined areas of shell are worked in horizontal gobelin stitch with twelve strands of white floss in needle; all other areas of shell and stripes in background are worked in continental stitch with twelve strands of floss; black background is worked in continental stitch using mat finished cotton.

Brown-Striped Voluta Shell: Striped brown areas of shell are worked in horizontal gobelin stitch using mat finished cotton; the rest of the shell is worked in continental stitch, also with mat finished cotton. The background is worked in continental stitch using twelve strands embroidery floss.

Purple Murex Shell: The entire shell and all stripes in background are worked in contintental stitch, using six-strand embroidery floss. The remaining white background areas are worked in brick stitch, using mat finished cotton.

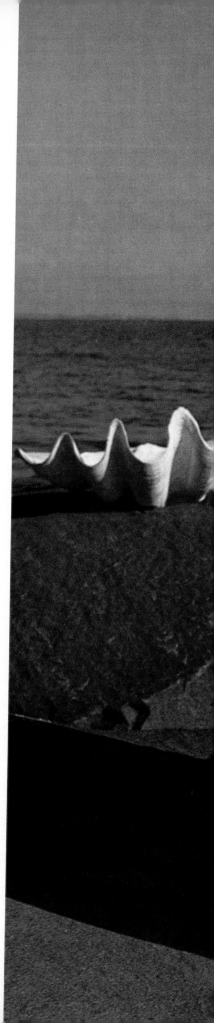

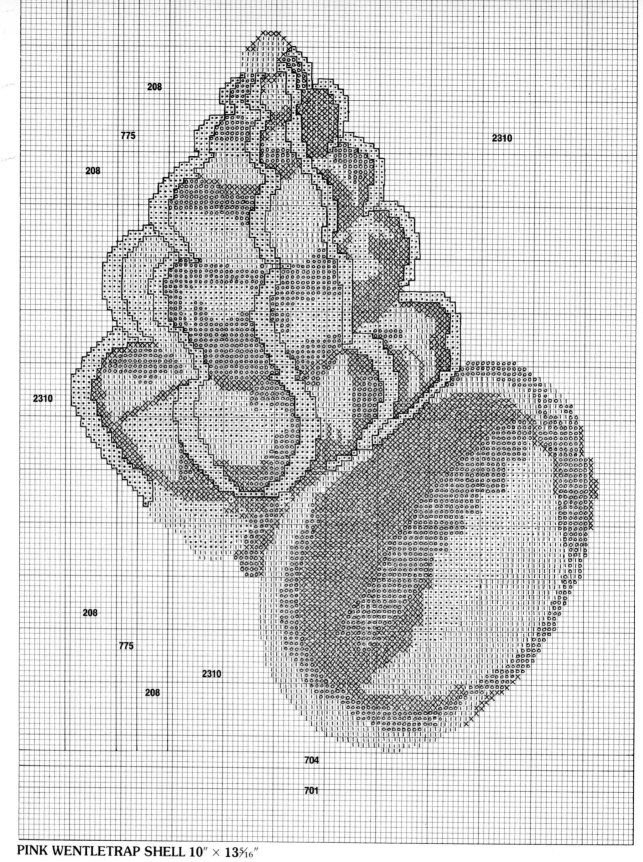

PINK WENTLETRAP SHELL 10″ × 13⁵⁄₁₆″

Color	D.M.C Embroidery Floss	Skeins		Color	D.M.C Embroidery Floss	Skeins
☒ Dark pink	605	6		Purple	208	6
⊙ Medium pink	818	6		Light blue	775	2
Ⅱ Light pink	819	6		**D.M.C Mat-Finished Cotton**		
· White	Snow white	10				
Dark green	701	6				
Light green	704	2		Black	2310	10

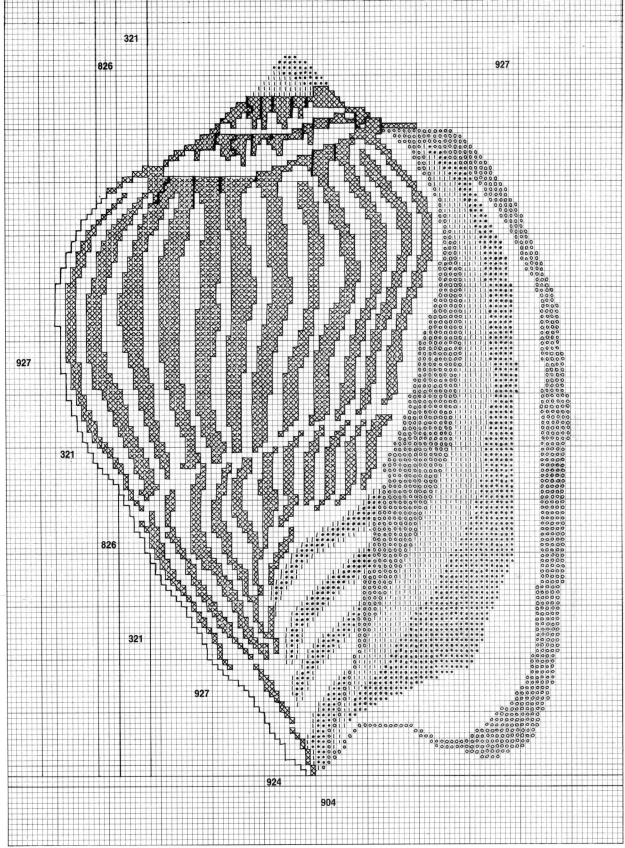

BROWN-STRIPED VOLUTA SHELL 10″ × 13⁵⁄₁₆″

Color	D.M.C Mat-Finished Cotton	Skeins		Color	D.M.C Embroidery Floss	Skeins
☒ Dark brown	2299	3		Red	321	6
⊡ Medium brown	2405	2		Dark green	924	2
⊞ Light brown	2407	1		Blue	826	2
⊡ Beige	2950	2		Pale green	927	20
☐ White	Blanc	5		Medium green	904	6

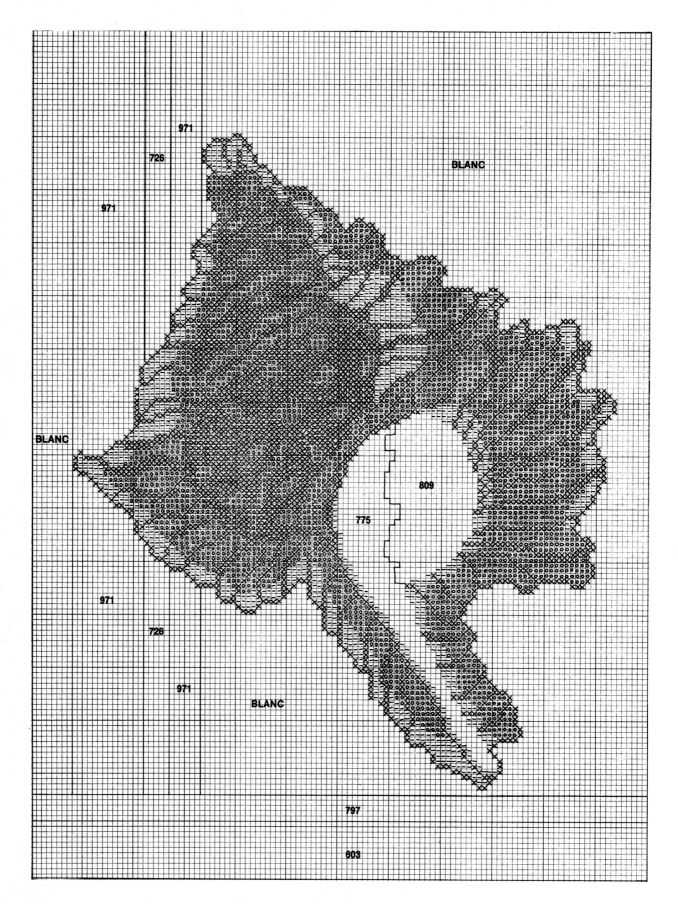

971
726
BLANC
971
BLANC
971
726
971
BLANC
775
809
797
603

152

◄ PURPLE MUREX SHELL 10″ × 13⅚₆″

Color	D.M.C Embroidery Floss	Skeins
☒ Dark purple	208	16
⊡ Medium purple	209	14
⊟ Light purple	211	10
Dark blue	797	4
Medium blue	809	4
Light blue	775	4
Rose	603	6
Yellow	726	4
Orange	971	16

	D.M.C Mat-Finished Cotton	
White	Blanc	5

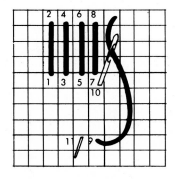

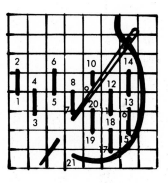

GOBELIN STITCH

Work first row with upright vertical stitches from left to right, going over the number of meshes required to make stitch desired length. Work second row of stitches directly below first row, going from right to left. Keep yarn flat and untwisted, employing a little less tension than usual, so rows of stitches will have a slightly puffy or quilted look. The gobelin stitch is usually worked in rows of equal-length stitches, but where used in these pictures, stitch lengths vary to follow the design lines of the shells. The stitch is always worked in upright position; to work horizontal rows, turn the canvas.

BRICK STITCH

The brick stitch is a variation of the upright gobelin stitch, and again, length of stitches can vary. In white background of purple shell picture, stitches are all the same length. Work first stitch over two meshes of canvas; bring needle out to right one mesh below first stitch. Again work stitch over two meshes; bring needle out to right one mesh above second stitch. Continue across row, alternating stitches up and down to create "brick" pattern. On next row, work from right to left, with top of stitches in same holes as bottom of stitches in first row.

SCULPTURE FROM THE SEA

Only nature could create the infinite variety of shapes found in over 100,000 different species of shells, but you can take advantage of her sea-born artworks. Here, easy ways to spotlight their beauty.

A variety of shells (plus one small sea creature) are simply glued to the corks of glass containers.

Tiny, vividly hued shells are glued to a small piece of coral, natural habitat of many mollusks.

Any shell with a deep aperture can be used to hold fresh or dried flowers. Fit foam or Plasticine inside to hold stems of dried flowers in place.

A Voluta imperialis, *king of crown-shaped shells, is starkly beautiful as a piece of wood-based sculpture.*

WOOD-BASED
SHELL SCULPTURE

MATERIALS NEEDED
  Voluta imperialis shell, 5″ to 6″ high
  Brass rod or heavy coat hanger wire, about 12″
  3 x 3 lumber, 5″ length
  Walnut stain
  Glue

Sand and stain wood for mounting block. Mark center of top surface of block; using wood bit, drill a hole about halfway down length of block. Using masonry bit, drill hole in "crown" end of shell as close to center as possible. Apply glue to end of rod; push into coiled interior of shell as far as it will go. Allow glue to dry. Allowing for insertion into wood plus 3½″ to 4″ which will show, cut off any excess rod. Apply glue and push rod into hole in block.

THE
HOLIDAY
SEASON

A
TREE
TO
REMEMBER...
MAKE
IT
FOR
KEEPS

The symbol of Christmas for many centuries, a gaily decorated tree casts a spell of enchantment on the whole holiday season. A towering Christmas tree fresh from the forest and laden with sparkling new ornaments is a splendid sight to behold. But there's even more magic in a tree that's a family tradition, decorated with memories as well as baubles, and brought forth with nostalgic excitement year after year. Gloria Vanderbilt's version of just such a memory tree is seen below, small but resplendent, packed with all manner of miniature trinkets and treasures, many older than either of her two young sons. Opposite, an updated version you can duplicate: all the mini-ornaments are widely available, including the Christmas cutouts from pages 168 and 169, tiny flowers from a millinery store, gilt decoupage cutouts from any craft shop, miniature pots, pans, musical instruments and delicacies designed for dollhouses, diminutive Christmas-tree balls and glittery dangles made of gift-wrapping cord. Directions on how to begin follow—but be sure to add your own memory-filled family mementos year after happy year.

MATERIALS NEEDED

18"-tall Styrofoam cone
Green spray paint
Artificial green foliage, enough to cover cone
Metal, plastic or wood miniatures and trinkets
Tiny artificial flowers and buds in pastel colors
Small artificial red roses
Paper cutouts from pages 168 and 169
Purchased gilt paper cutouts
Tiny Christmas-tree balls, varied sizes and colors
Lightweight wire
Five boxes of long hairpins
Metallic gift-wrapping cord in assorted colors
Double-faced Scotch tape
Small wicker basket, about 6" in diameter
6" cube of Styrofoam, or enough scraps to fill basket
7"-long dowel, ½" diameter
Small, heavy pebbles
White glue

Spray cone with green paint. Place a layer of pebbles in bottom of basket. Cut piece of Styrofoam to fit snugly inside basket to just below top edge, or pack basket tightly with Styrofoam scraps. Apply glue to both ends of dowel and insert one end into exact center of Styrofoam in basket. Insert other end into center of base of tree, leaving about 1" of dowel between top of basket and tree.

Starting at base of cone and working upward to about 3" from tip, cover cone completely with pieces of green foliage; use pieces 4" to 6" long, bend each one in half around rounded end of hairpin, and push straight ends of hairpin into Styrofoam cone. Cover the tip of cone with smallest flowers, attaching them in the same manner.

When cone is completely covered with foliage and tiny flowers, add miniatures, trinkets, small red roses, small Christmas-tree balls and other ornaments, starting with largest objects at bottom of tree and graduating sizes so smallest are near the top, attaching them all with hairpins.

To make cone-shaped dangles from metallic gift-wrapping cord, first cut 7"-lengths of wire and bend each in half into a loop. Twist the two cut ends together and shape wire into narrow cone. Using two colors of metallic cord together, start at twisted ends of wire and wrap cord diagonally around wire up to wider curved end. Secure cord in place by twisting around curved end of wire and insert hairpin through loop to attach dangle to tree.

Add paper cutouts last; attach each cutout to rounded end of hairpin with small piece of double-faced tape and push straight ends of hairpin into tree so cutout is poised at edge of foliage and other trims.

A DOZEN DECORATING IDEAS TO BRIGHTEN THE HOLIDAYS

1

Tie up a white or glass-topped table with wide red satin ribbon and the simplest meal will look like an exciting Christmas package. You can tape the ribbon in place under the tabletop and wire a few Christmas-tree balls and some sprigs of greenery to the bow for an unusual centerpiece. Carry the idea even further and tie a long-streamered bow to the back of each chair. It's an easy and inexpensive way to decorate for a Christmas party.

2

Adapt a colorful Swedish custom and do your Christmas decorating with bright red apples. In this case, the "apples" are made of red ribbon topped with tiny green felt leaves. They dangle at different heights from a wreath of fragrant evergreens studded with little red berries. The wreath is suspended from the ceiling with more red ribbon. We filled each "apple" with a shiny Christmas-tree ball to make it even more colorful, and the total effect is very festive. More details on page 166.

3

If you're lucky enough to have a fireplace with a mantel, make the most of it during the holidays. It can be a warm and welcoming focal point when decorated with a miniature gift-tree loaded with candy canes and edible goodies for young visitors. Under the tree goes an array of gaily wrapped small gift boxes, each holding a tiny bottle of Christmas cheer or a few special confections you made yourself—maybe brandy-soaked dates, or brandy-soaked prunes decorated with blanched almonds, each in a fluted paper candy cup. Have enough of the little gifts wrapped and ready so that no guest goes away empty-handed during the holiday season.

4

Festive table dressing without fuss or bother—it takes little or no sewing, and no handwork at all. Start with a circle (or a rectangle or a square, depending on your table) of Christmas-red felt and top with any white lace cloth in your linen closet— also round or square, or what-have-you? You don't? How about a big, square, crocheted white shawl?

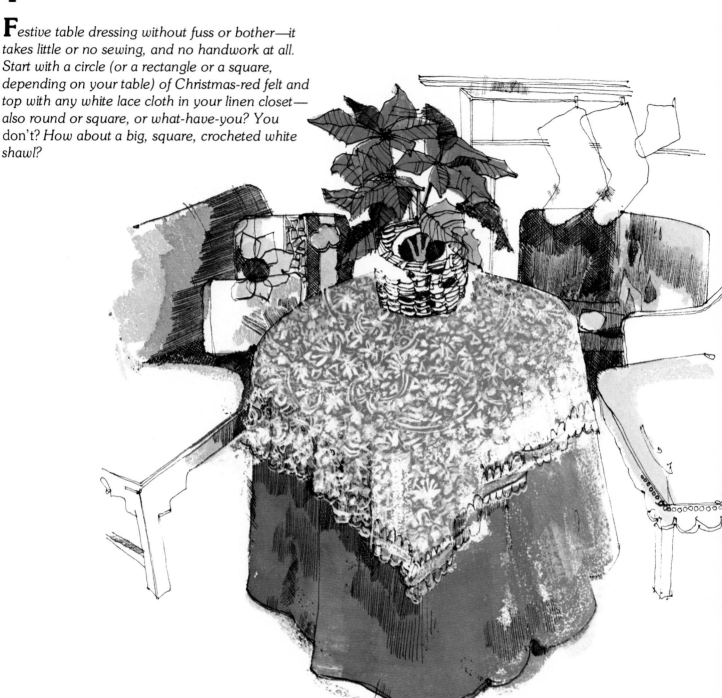

5

A Christmas "tree" doesn't have to be a tree. If your floor space is limited, use garlands of evergreens, trimmed or untrimmed, all over the house. In a small, square dining room, for instance, drape a rope of greenery into scallops around the walls at the ceiling line—rather like a bordered wallpaper. Wire with tiny white Christmas-tree lights for spectacular sparkle, or just add small, shiny Christmas-tree balls nestled in the greenery. And greens twisted around and through a chandelier always look great, too. Or frame a large mirror with light-studded greens.

6

Instead of (or in addition to) one huge Christmas tree, why not a whole series of miniatures—one for every room in the house? In a feminine bedroom, trim with festoons of fake pearls tied on with tiny pink velvet bows. In a child's room, swingy mobiles cut from brightly colored paper. In the kitchen, walnuts and plastic fruit painted gold and silver.

7

No room for a Christmas tree in your tiny apartment? Have one anyway—and a perennial one at that. Cut a stylized tree from green felt, tape it to a wall, and trim exactly as you would the real thing—shiny balls, glittery baubles, candy canes, the whole bit. And don't forget a bright red tub to stand it in—also of felt. Come Twelfth Night, take it all down and roll the tree up, ready for next year.

8

A kissing ring that doesn't mince words about its mission in life—even though it's pretty enough to be pure decoration. A wreath of Christmas greenery is suspended by pink satin ribbons and dotted with rosettes of ruffled eyelet embroidery. Sprigs of mistletoe dangle from a beribboned double rosette. See page 167 for easy directions.

9

The simplest of centerpieces will add double sparkle to a holiday table. Group a dozen or more fat red candles, each one a different height, in the center of an oval mirror, and wreath the edge of the mirror with sprigs of Christmas greenery. The rosy glow of the candles and their flickering, dancing lights will be reflected in the mirror, adding a fairyland touch to any table.

10

Trim a whole Christmas tree with bows of red-and-white gingham, starting with tiny bows in minuscule checks at the top of the tree and graduating to bigger bows in the largest checks you can find (usually 1" size) toward the bottom. Wrap all the packages that go under the tree in red-and-white checks as well, and tie with solid red or green ribbon. If you don't feel like cutting and stitching strips of fabric to make bows, look for checked taffeta ribbon, which can sometimes be found in both red-and-white and green-and-white and would make bright, perky bows.

11

Encourage your children to create Christmas "paintings" in crayon or poster paint—nativity scenes, Christmas trees, Santa and/or his reindeer, whatever symbolizes, to them, the excitement of the season—and install in inexpensive red and green frames from the dime store. Take down, temporarily, the paintings, prints and wall hangings that decorate your rooms and cover the walls with the joyous works of your offspring. With a minimum of encouragement, you'll have artworks galore!

12

A high-spirited centerpiece for a festive Christmas Day dinner (or an even more festive New Year's Eve supper) is also a fitting finale for the repast. Hang tiny bottles of liqueurs from a miniature man-made Christmas tree with brightly colored ribbons and let each guest pluck his or her choice from a varied assortment of familiar favorites and exotic new flavors.

13

It's a baker's dozen! The thirteenth (and most important) decorating idea is—decorate yourself. To do so effectively, you'll need time and rest and a relaxed frame of mind, so do your holiday decorating early, and have a wonderful time!

RIBBON AND EVERGREEN "APPLE" RING

MATERIALS NEEDED

Inside circle of 12"-diameter embroidery hoop
9 yards red grosgrain ribbon, 1" wide
7½" yards red grosgrain ribbon, ⅝" wide
¾ yard emerald or apple green ribbon, ⅜" wide
Scraps of green felt
8 Christmas-tree balls, 3½" diameter: silver, gold, shocking pink, purple (or desired colors)
Evergreen branches
Artificial red holly berries
Florists' wire
White glue
Wooden spring-type clothespins

Each red "apple" that holds a Christmas-tree ball is formed by three strips of red grosgrain ribbon; four "apples" are made of 1"-wide ribbon, the other four are made of ⅝"-wide ribbon. For each "apple," cut three 12"-long strips of ribbon. Place strips in three directions with centers overlapping; glue together where they overlap (Diagram 1).

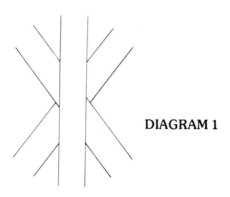

DIAGRAM 1

When glue is dry, glue free ends together in same manner to form apple shape; secure joining with clothespin until glue is thoroughly dry.

From green felt, cut eight 1"-diameter circles with zigzag edges for "leaves." Glue one "leaf" on top of each "apple" where ribbons are glued together. Secure with clothespin until dry.

Cut eight 3"-long strips of green grosgrain ribbon. Overlap ends as shown in Diagram 2 and glue together. Secure with clothespin until dry, then glue one loop of green ribbon to center of "leaf" on top of each "apple."

DIAGRAM 2

Cut eight strips of the ⅝"-wide red ribbon in varying lengths from 6" to 16". Fold one end of each strip to form a point and glue to top of "apple" where ends of green loop overlap. Glue the other end of each strip to the inside of the hoop so the "apples" hang down, spacing the eight strips at equal intervals around the circle.

Cut four 35" lengths of the 1"-wide grosgrain ribbon; glue to inside of hoop at equal intervals so the hoop hangs down. (Space these ribbons between ribbons holding "apples.") Tie the four loose ends together in a bow.

Glue a strip of wide grosgrain ribbon around outside of hoop; glue a strip of narrow grosgrain ribbon around inside of hoop. Clip with clothespins between ribbons and allow glue to dry thoroughly.

Wire evergreen branches around outside of hoop, with all branches going in same direction. Glue small twigs of greenery around inside of hoop to hide wire. Stick stems of artificial holly berries into branches all around hoop. Slide a Christmas-tree ball into each "apple" and hang hoop from bow.

KISSING RING

MATERIALS NEEDED

1 wire wreath frame or wire coat hanger
6 yards pink satin ribbon, 1″ or 1½″ wide
2 yards eyelet ruffling with hemmed heading, 1½″ wide
1 small spool of lightweight, covered wire
Sprigs of holly or laurel
Sprigs of mistletoe
1 pipe cleaner

If using wire coat hanger to make ring, cut off curved hook and shape triangular base into a circle to make frame. Cut four 18″ lengths of pink ribbon; fasten one end of each around frame, spacing them equally around circle. Attach sprigs of holly or laurel to frame with small strips of covered wire, forming a wreath.

Cut seven 8″ lengths of pink ribbon and tie each into a small bow; cut ends into inverted V's. Twist a 6″-long piece of wire around center of each bow several times, leaving free ends about 2½″ long.

Cut seven 9″-long strips of eyelet ruffling and seven 10″-long strips of covered wire. Fold one end of each wire back on itself to make smooth, looped end and thread through hemmed heading of eyelet strip. Gather ruffling tightly in center of wire and shape into small ring so eyelet ruffling forms a circle. Twist ends of wire tightly together where ends of ruffling meet (see Diagram). Fasten a ribbon bow to center of each eyelet circle by tacking to ruffling.

Cut a length of ribbon approximately 24″ long. Place wreath on flat surface and gather loose ends of four ribbons from which it will be suspended together, with end of longer ribbon in the center so it will hang down through center of wreath. Stitch ends of all five ribbons together, then twist pipe cleaner very securely around fastened ends and form a loop hook with remainder of pipe cleaner. Slip a ruffled circle with bow down over pipe-cleaner hook; insert sprigs of laurel or holly and add more bows if desired. Hang loop on a nail or hook and make sure wreath hangs level.

Fasten a ruffled circle to outside of wreath at base of each ribbon from which wreath is suspended. Add sprigs of greenery as desired (see photograph). Place two remaining ruffled circles back to back and add sprigs of mistletoe on both sides, twisting ends of wires on which ruffling is gathered around stems of mistletoe. Tie several pink ribbon bows around stems and staple to end of ribbon hanging freely in center of wreath.

CHRISTMAS CUTOUTS

Cutouts, without printing on the back, are repeated at the back of this book.

COMPLIMENTS OF THE SEASON.

MERRY CHRISTMAS

CHRISTMAS
CUTOUTS
GLAMORIZE
SMALL
GIFTS

The small gift you make yourself for stocking stuffer or "extra" can express a loving thought as effectively as the most expensive present. The colorful Christmas cutouts, carefully reproduced from old prints that are hard to find today, make it easy to transform ordinary objects into charming and personalized mementos.

Frame one of the jolly Santas on page 169 and let him carry your greeting to someone special in lieu of a conventional Christmas card. Brightly outlined in red and green ribbon, he'll make quite a splash—and reappear every holiday season. You hardly need directions for these easy-to-duplicate ideas, but we've spelled them out anyway; see page 172.

A mundane box of kitchen matches can be proudly displayed when camouflaged by a delightfully decorated metal "slipcover" that costs less than two dollars. The cutouts, some self-adhesive "velour," bits of velvet ribbon and gold paper braid are all it takes. Next to it, above, a nondescript little cube that was transformed into a very decorative objet by much the same treatment.

SANTA CLAUS PICTURE

MATERIALS NEEDED

Small picture frame, 5½" x 7" or smaller
¾ yard green velvet ribbon, ¼" wide
½ yard red velvet ribbon, ¼" wide
Scrap of off-white felt or other fabric
Santa Claus cutout from page 169
Cardboard
Masking tape
White glue

Picture frame shown, which is wide for its 5½" x 7" size, gives maximum importance to small Santa Claus cutout. If frame selected is narrower, overall size should be smaller.

Cut cardboard to fit into rabbet of frame. Cut felt or other fabric 2" wider and 2" longer than cardboard; center cardboard on wrong side of fabric, wrap 1" allowance around edges of cardboard and glue to back, clipping fabric diagonally at corners and cutting away excess. Cut strips of green velvet ribbon to fit just inside front opening of frame and glue in place on covered cardboard, mitering corners. Cut strips of red velvet ribbon to fit and glue in place approximately ³⁄₁₆" from inside edges of green ribbon, mitering corners. Center cutout inside ribbon and glue in place. Place glass in frame (if covering picture with glass), insert picture and secure to back of frame with masking tape. If desired, cut piece of brown paper to same size as frame and glue to back edges of frame to conceal tape.

MATCHBOX COVER

MATERIALS NEEDED

Metal "slipcover" for box of kitchen matches
1 sheet of hot pink velour-finish "Peel and Pat"
¾ yard fuchsia grosgrain ribbon, ⅜" wide
¼ yard moss green velvet ribbon, ¼" wide
Paper cutouts from page 168
1 strip each of two different gold paper braids
Gilt or silver paint
White glue

NOTE: "Peel and Pat" is a self-adhesive paper with protective peel-off backing which comes in several finishes and is available at craft and hobby shops. The type used here has a "velour-feel" finish which looks and feels like velveteen.

Cut piece of "Peel and Pat" slightly larger than size required to cover metal matchbox holder. (Holder shown has rounded top; some are made with flat top to fit over standard box of kitchen matches exactly.) Peel off protective backing and smooth over metal holder. Trim excess along edges. Paste any loose edges down by applying glue with a toothpick. Cut four strips of fuchsia grosgrain ribbon to width of holder, usually 5", and glue in place where top begins to curve, back and front, and to bottom edges. Glue narrow gold paper braid just below grosgrain ribbon on front and around other three edges. Cut two 2½" strips of green velvet ribbon and glue along side edges just inside braid. Cut two 2½" strips of wider gold paper braid and glue close to inside edges of green ribbon. Glue paper cutouts in place (see photo). Apply glue to ribbon, braid and cutouts, not to covered holder; avoid getting glue on holder by wiping hands frequently with damp paper towels. Back of holder can be decorated in similar manner or left plain.

Paint sides of box that the matches come in with gilt or silver paint and slide box into holder.

DECORATED CUBE

MATERIALS NEEDED

1 cube, 4" square
¼ yard beige felt (or suitable scraps)
2¼ yards gold grosgrain ribbon, ¼" wide
1½ yards violet grosgrain ribbon, ¼" wide
3 strips narrow gold paper braid
4 strips wider gold paper braid
Paper cutouts from pages 168 and 169
White glue

Cut one 4" x 16" piece of felt and two 4" x 4" pieces. Wrapping 16"-long piece around four sides of cube, glue it to one side at a time. Glue 4"-square pieces to top and bottom. Trim any excess along edges.

Cut twenty 4"-long strips of gold ribbon and glue along all edges of sides and top of cube, mitering the corners by cutting the ribbon diagonally after gluing each strip in place so the mitered strips butt precisely.

Cut twenty 3½"-long strips of the wider gold paper braid and glue in place along inside edges of the gold ribbon. Cut twenty 2¾"-long strips of the narrow paper braid and glue in place close to the wider braid strips. Cut twenty 2½"-long strips of violet ribbon and glue in place just inside narrow paper braid, mitering the corners in same manner as before. Glue paper cutout in center of braid-and-ribbon "frame" on each side of cube, using five different motifs to make cube interesting. Apply glue to ribbon, braid and cutouts, not to cube; avoid getting glue on cube by wiping hands frequently with damp paper towels.

GIFT-WRAP ART: CUTOUTS MAKE EACH PACKAGE A MINI-COLLAGE

Don't spend your precious time wrapping Christmas packages that look like everyone else's. All it takes to do something different are the cutouts on pages 168 and 169—plus a little imagination. Here, just a few ideas to get you started.

Cut up some lacy paper place mats from your local five-and-ten (or use ones you have on hand) and add a sprinkling of colorful cutouts for feminine collage-wraps like the ones opposite. You can recolor the silvery butterflies to go with your color scheme.

You can forget the usual ribbons and bows (especially for his packages) when you have such a variety of cutouts. The bright little clocks, for instance, are a clever clue to a gift watch. And with "Merry Christmas" spelled out, you don't even need a card!

CREATE A CHRISTMAS GARDEN

Grow flowers for Christmas—in colorful stained glass. These inventive indoor "gardens" will lend a holiday glow to any setting—contemporary or traditional. The opaque white glass oval in the window garden opposite can be used to express any sentiment you like, via press-on type or glued-on gold paper letters.

The candle garden below makes a glowing holiday decoration—and a delightfully appropriate centerpiece all spring and summer. You can "grow" the flowers to suit your own color scheme, or plan the colors to please someone special on your gift list.

GENERAL DIRECTIONS FOR STAINED-GLASS PROJECTS

MATERIALS NEEDED (for either project)

36-yard roll of copper foil tape with adhesive backing, ¼″ wide

Liquid oleic acid soldering flux

Whiting powder (powdered chalk)

1-pound spool of solid wire solder, 60/40

Household oil, a small amount

Scraps of glass for practice

Copper sulfate antiquing solution

Glass and other materials listed in specific directions (Amounts of glass listed are only approximate, since some breakage is inevitable)

You'll also need carbon paper, heavy paper for patterns, all-purpose glue, a glass cutter with tapping ball, glass breakers, grozing pliers for honing glass edges, needle-nosed wire-cutting pliers, a small, stiff-bristle acid brush, a soldering iron with flat or pyramid top (40 watts), an orange stick, cotton swabs, liquid glass cleaner, a clean, empty tin can, paper towels, newspapers, rags and eyeglasses or plastic goggles.

Before working on glass for projects, practice cutting and soldering on scraps. Cover working surface with newspaper to avoid spreading glass dust. Wear glasses or goggles for protection. Before beginning, pour small amount of oil into tin can.

Enlarge patterns to actual size on paper ruled in 1″ squares and number each piece of glass in design. Using carbon paper, trace patterns, including numbers, onto heavy paper and cut out individual numbered pieces. Place patterns on glass and lightly glue in place; use a ruler as a guide for straight lines.

To cut glass along pattern edges, first score glass with cutter, drawing cutter toward you in one firm, continuous motion. Do not go over scored line;

doing so dulls cutter and can cause an uneven break. If cutter works stiffly, dip it in household oil. Break glass along scored lines in following manner: For straight edges, grasp glass firmly at each side of score and bend downward and outward, pressing evenly. For curved edges, tap once directly beneath score with ball end of glass cutter, then break glass away. Snip off any jagged edges with glass breakers, then hone edges with grozing pliers so glass matches outline of pattern.

When you have cut all glass pieces needed for one design, follow numbers to arrange pieces over original enlarged pattern to make sure pieces fit properly. If necessary, hone edges again to make them fit better. Remove patterns from glass pieces, but keep glass in place on top of original enlarged pattern. Wrap copper foil tape evenly around edges of each piece by placing edge in center of strip of tape with an equal amount of tape extending on each side. Overlap ends of tape about ¼″ where they meet and cut tape. Wrap edges of tape tightly around edges of glass. Flatten tape against glass by pressing down with orange stick to make certain it is secure. Check fit again.

When all pieces have been wrapped, remove original pattern. With pieces in place, brush flux over all copper foil surfaces with stiff-bristle brush. Continue brushing frequently during soldering process. Make sure working area is well ventilated before beginning soldering.

If soldering iron has never been used, the copper tip must be tinned. Heat iron, brush tip with flux and apply a small amount of solder. Solder adheres to the copper, not to the glass. If solder drops on glass, let it cool and brush off. To solder, hold heated tip of soldering iron close to copper and apply end of solder wire to iron, letting solder flow down tip onto copper. First, spot solder at several points to hold pieces together; then solder pieces together by drawing iron along copper tape, spreading solder. Do not allow soldering iron to remain at any point for more than an instant, since heat may make glass break. Solder pieces together on front and let cool; solder together on back and let cool. Continue soldering until all copper is covered. When soldering edges, pieces can be held upright with pliers. Repeat soldering process if necessary; all copper must be covered.

When completely cool, sprinkle whiting powder on piece and wipe off with cloth to remove excess flux oil. Wash piece until solder is shiny and glass is clean, then dry.

To antique, apply copper sulfate solution to solder with a cotton swab; rub with cloth until solder appears dark or brassy. Let dry, wash with glass cleaner, then rinse and dry.

WINDOW GARDEN

MATERIALS NEEDED
(in addition to those listed in general directions)
    Cathedral glass:
        8″ square of each color to be used in flowers (As shown: gold, bright yellow, pale yellow, lavender, violet, purple)
    10″ squares of medium green and dark green
    White opaque glass, 11″ x 14″
    Press-on-type or gold paper letters
    Thin, nickel-plated copper wire, 8″ long, for loops
    Nylon filament, 50-pound test, for hanging

Pattern is given in two sections; join enlarged sections along broken lines to make complete pattern.

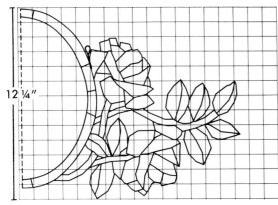

12¼″

1 square = 1″

Cut center oval from white glass. Following general directions, cut and assemble pieces for flowers, stems and oval frame. See photograph for color arrangement of flowers, or use colors desired. Use medium green for half of each leaf, dark green for the other half. Cut pieces for oval frame from dark green glass.

To make loops for hanging, cut two 4″ lengths of wire. Fold each in half, forming a small loop. Placement of loops is indicated in heavy line on pattern. Place loops on edge between top flowers and oval frame as indicated and solder ends in place. Cut two pieces of nylon filament to desired length; thread through loops to hang piece.

CANDLE GARDEN

MATERIALS NEEDED
(in addition to those listed in general directions)
    Cathedral glass:
        6″ square of each color to be used in flowers (As shown: gold, bright yellow, pale yellow, bright blue, dark blue, purple)
    12″ x 14″ piece of yellow-green for base, stem and leaves
    10″ squares of medium green and dark green for remaining stems and leaves

Garden is composed of eleven flowers on stems of varying heights. Patterns for two different flowers are given; the simpler one may be used for all flowers, or other slight variations added. Following general directions, cut and assemble pieces for flower petals and centers.

Cut 8½″-diameter round base from yellow-green glass; wrap edge with copper foil tape. Using all

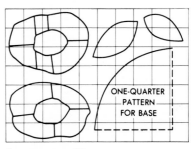

ONE-QUARTER PATTERN FOR BASE

1 square = 1″

three shades of green, cut eleven straight pieces across width of glass for stems, each ½" wide. When ready to assemble, strips can be cut to desired lengths. Using both leaf patterns, cut leaves from various shades of green as needed to fill areas between stems.

To begin assembling "garden," cut one stem 7" long. Following general directions, attach flower at top of stem and leaves in desired positions. Holding flower and stem upright, solder bottom of stem to top surface of base, flush with edge of base; prop up while attaching next stem to base. Leaves or flowers on adjacent stems must touch, and be soldered to, at least one leaf or flower of preceding stem for support. Cut stems in lengths required to make flowers and leaves support each other. Place stems from 2½" to 3½" apart around base. To vary heights and place some flowers low enough to support other stems, attach flower to short stem and continue stem above it, attaching another flower or more leaves (see photograph). Tallest flower or leaf should be about 11½" above base.

White, self-standing candles can be placed directly on base to illuminate garden, but standing candles in a shallow metal lid painted to match base is recommended.

SOME OF GLORIA'S FAVORITE GIFTS

SLEEPYHEAD PILLOW

Many of the projects in this book make super-gifts, but some of Gloria's own favorites are charming trifles you can whip up in no time. Witness this whimsical little pillow—a tiny 3½" x 6½" of machine-embroidered velveteen that makes an amusing (and very practical) present for any traveler or perennial sleepyhead.

MATERIALS NEEDED
Solid-color velveteen, 8" x 9"
1 yard rayon cable cord, ¼" diameter
Thread to match cord
Polyester fiberfill
Tracing paper
Dressmakers' tracing paper

Enlarge pattern for embroidery onto paper ruled in ½" squares and trace full-size lettering. From velveteen, cut two 4½" x 7½" rectangles. Using dressmakers' tracing paper, transfer embroidery pattern to one piece of velveteen, centering it on right side of rectangle. Satin-stitch embroidery can be done by hand, or by machine using close zigzag stitch. Stitch directly over single lines and between double lines of lettering.

Cut a 7" length of cord for handle. Place cord on right side of embroidered rectangle, with ends extending ½" above top edge of velveteen at a point 1¼" in from each side edge. Place second rectangle over embroidered one with right sides together and edges even, enclosing all but extending ends of cord. Stitch rectangles together ½" from edges, stitching over cord and leaving a 3" opening at center of bottom edge. Trim seam allowances to ¼". Turn right side out and stuff plumply with fiberfill. Slipstitch opening closed except for ½".

Cut a 22" length of cord, center on seam line at top of pillow, and pin along seam line all around pillow. Slipstitch cord in place, inserting ends into opening at bottom; slipstitch opening closed.

PATTERN FOR EMBROIDERY

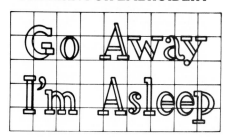

1 square = ½"

LINGERIE CASES

A trio of lingerie cases bordered with ribbon-beaded eyelet and lined with polka dots—what could be more like Gloria? Three different sizes make pretty hideaways for everything from panty hose to full-length nightgowns, and will make your favorite traveler feel pampered and luxurious en route or at home.

MATERIALS NEEDED
(for three cases: 13" x 16"; 11¼" x 13"; 9" x 10")
- ¾ yard printed fabric, 44" wide
- 1¼ yards polka-dotted fabric, 44" wide
- 1½ yards color-coordinated lining fabric, 44" wide
- Color-coordinated thread
- 9 yards satin ribbon, ⅜" wide
- 5¼ yards white embroidered eyelet beading, 1" wide
- 1 layer polyester batting, 30" x 36"

Large- and medium-size cases are made with a single pocket in polka-dotted fabric to match lining; small case has two additional pockets of lightweight lining fabric.

For large case, cut one piece of printed fabric and one piece of polka-dotted fabric, each 17" x 26¾". For pocket, cut one piece of polka-dotted fabric and one of lining fabric, 11¾" x 17". Cut a piece of batting 15½" x 25¼".

Press ½" to wrong side all around both fabrics for case. With batting centered between them, pin and then baste printed and dotted fabrics together, wrong sides facing and edges even. Stitch together with diagonal quilting lines, starting and stopping ⅝" from all edges.

With right sides together, stitch dotted fabric for pocket to lining fabric along one long edge; turn right sides out and press. Stitch together around three remaining sides, ½" from raw edges; turn seam allowances to lining side and press. Pin lining side of pocket to polka-dotted side of case, with three edges even. Tuck ½" seam allowances of pocket between dotted and printed edges of case; baste through all four layers. Top-stitch around edges through all thicknesses.

Cut 74" lengths of satin ribbon and eyelet beading; thread ribbon through eyelets. Pin ribbon-beaded trimming around printed side of case, 1¼" in from edges, mitering corners and turning cut ends under. Blindstitch to case along both edges, catching only the printed fabric in stitching.

Cut two 31" lengths of ribbon. Fold cut end of

one to wrong side; with right side out, make a double loop, taking up 1¼", then 1". Tack together at side edges, then stitch to flap at center of edge. Repeat with second length of ribbon and stitch to center of bottom edge. Tie in a bow (see photograph).

For medium-size case, cut 23½" x 14" pieces of printed fabric and dotted fabric. For pocket, cut 10" x 14" pieces of dotted fabric and lining fabric. Cut batting 12½" x 22". Make case in same manner as large case. Cut 63" lengths of ribbon and eyelet beading. Apply to case 1" from edges. Use 20" lengths of ribbon for ties.

For small case, cut 11" x 19" pieces of printed fabric and dotted fabric. For first pocket, cut 8½" x 11" pieces of dotted fabric and lining fabric. For two additional pockets, cut two pieces of lining fabric, each 11" x 31". Cut batting 9½" x 17½".

Make small case with first pocket in same manner as large case. Cut 49" lengths of ribbon and eyelet beading; apply to case ⅞" from edges. Use 18" lengths of ribbon for ties.

To make two additional pockets of lining fabric, fold each rectangle in half horizontally, then bring folded edge up to ½" from cut edges. Stitch through all four layers of fabric along sides. Stitch through two layers of fabric across cut ends, leaving an opening for turning. Turn to right side and slipstitch opening closed. Top-stitch around entire folded top edge.

Place the two pockets together with all edges even. Edge-stitch the two adjoining open edges together, starting and stopping ½" from side edges. Place the joined pockets on polka-dotted pocket of case, all edges even; pin adjoining pockets together and edge-stitch as before.

PAPER PORTFOLIOS

Now, *about that person on your list who "has everything." We'll wager she doesn't have enough (if any) good-looking portfolios for all those endless papers and bills and letters on her desk. Wouldn't she love to have lots of fabric-lined folders in handsome endpapers like these? You could make a whole dozen—one for every month—for very little money. Where to find the endpapers? See page 223.*

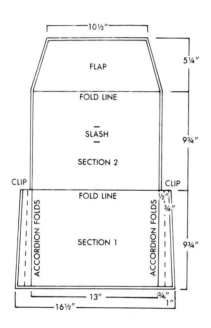

MATERIALS NEEDED

(for each 9¾" x 13" portfolio)

1 sheet patterned endpaper, at least 17" x 25"

½ yard solid-color linen or linen-textured fabric

1¼ yards grosgrain ribbon, approximately ⅝" wide

¾ yard fusible webbing, 21" wide

White glue

Paper for pattern

Masking tape

Enlarge pattern shown in diagram onto paper ruled in 1" squares. Mark ¼" margins, fold lines and ¾"-wide slash lines in Section 2. Cut out pattern and trace outline on wrong side of patterned endpaper; cut along outline.

Use same pattern to cut fabric lining and fusible webbing. Mark fold lines and slash lines on right side of fabric. Trim ¼" margins from fabric edges where marked on pattern. Center fabric over webbing, right side up, and pin in place. Trim edges of fusible webbing just inside edges of fabric.

Center fabric on wrong side of endpaper, webbing side down, with ¼" margins of paper extending beyond edges of fabric. Temporarily tape fabric to paper along margins, with four small pieces of tape. Pressing with steam or a wet cloth is usually recommended for fusing two fabrics together; *do not do so when fusing paper,* since dampness will cause most papers to buckle. Instead, press firmly with a hot, *dry* iron for a longer length of time than usual to fuse fabric to paper. When cool, cut through both thicknesses along slash lines. Clip into margins at two corners of Section 2 as indicated. Fold all margins of paper over edges of fabric and finger-press firmly, folding mitered corners; then glue to fabric, gluing side margins first and then margins at both ends.

With fabric side up, fold side edges of Section 1 toward center along solid lines, then fold outward along broken lines to form accordion pleats. Press pleats down firmly with a cool dry iron and dry press cloth. Cover turned-in margins of Section 1 and Section 2 with glue. Fold Section 1 over Section 2 along fold line; with side edges even, press down firmly to glue edges together. Fold flap over Section 1 along fold line. Place several heavy books on top of envelope until glue is thoroughly dry. Draw ribbon through slash lines on back of portfolio and tie in front.

PATCHWORK VEST

Gloria had this handsome patchwork vest made for her husband, who likes it both for festive affairs and for relaxing at home. Frankly luxurious, it's made of silky satin, velvet and ribbon patches in warm, rich colors—and looks especially dashing during the Christmas holidays. While it's definitely not for everyone, any man with a spark of romance in his soul will love it. Make one for yourself while you're about it; a vest like this is a long-term fashion investment.

MATERIALS NEEDED

Fabric scraps in a variety of colors and textures, such as satin, taffeta, velvet and brocade, in solid colors and patterns
Pattern for vest
1 yard lightweight fabric for lining, 44″ wide
Six-strand embroidery floss to match lining fabric
6 button molds, ½″ diameter
4 hooks and eyes
Lightweight cardboard

NOTE: Patchwork can be a "crazy quilt" of squares, rectangles, triangles and other shapes, or made mostly of squares, as in vest shown.

Patchwork is made in sections from which pattern pieces can be cut. To make patchwork, lay out scraps of fabric on a large, flat surface and arrange adjoining colors and textures for a pleasing effect, in either a random pattern or a geometric design. Cut scraps in desired shapes, allowing ¼″ seam allowance on all sides, so they can be stitched together into sections of the required size.

Vest shown has eight-pointed patchwork star worked into front sections of vest. Star is made of diamond-shaped patches, brown velvet on one side, brown satin on the other. To duplicate star, trace actual-size diamond pattern shown in Diagram 1 onto cardboard; add ¼″ seam allowance and cut out. Cut four complete diamonds for each side of front, plus a matching strip cut to dimensions shown in Diagram 2 (plus ¼″ seam allowance on all sides). Stitch pieces together by hand or machine as shown in diagram and place half-stars in patchwork layouts for front sections of vest, fitting contrasting patches between points. Stitch patchwork pieces for each section of vest together; press seams flat. With center front line of star matching center front line of pattern, pin and cut front sections of vest; then cut back sections. Stitch together

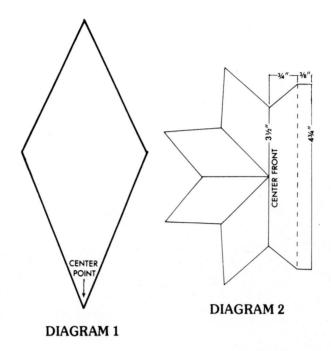

DIAGRAM 1

DIAGRAM 2

following pattern directions. Trim front edge ¾″ on left side for men, or right side for women. Machine-stitch ½″ in from raw edges.

Four flower motifs are embroidered on front of vest shown. Any motif desired could be used, placed symmetrically or scattered at random over entire vest. Turn ⅝″ seam allowance to wrong side around edges and armholes of vest, clipping ⅜″ into seam allowances around curves; baste in place. Cut lining and assemble in same manner as vest. Machine-stitch ¾″ in from all raw edges and clip around curves. Turn edges under on stitching line and pin lining to vest, wrong sides together, with turned edges of lining meeting stitching line on vest. Slipstitch lining to vest. Sew on four hooks and eyes or make "eyes" by hand in matching thread. Cover buttons following directions on package. Sew to vest ½″ in from edge.

TOWN
HOUSE
FOR RENT:

READY FOR
OCCUPANCY
DECEMBER 25

MATERIALS NEEDED

¼″ plywood, 4′ x 4′ half panel
Balsa wood stripping in following sizes:

¹⁄₁₆″ x ¹⁄₁₆″	⅛″ x ⅛″
¹⁄₁₆″ x ⅛″	⅛″ x ¼″
¹⁄₁₆″ x ¼″	⅛″ x ½″
¹⁄₁₆″ x ½″	¼″ x ¼″
¹⁄₁₆″ x ¾″	¼″ x ½″

1 piece ¹⁄₁₆″-thick balsa wood, 4″ x 8″
1 piece ⅛″-thick balsa wood, 4″ x 6″
2 metal hinges, 1¼″ maximum length
Acrylic paints: one small tube each yellow, white, dark gray, blue
Brown wood stain
6 sheets dollhouse wallpaper in varied patterns
Solid-color fabric or paper to coordinate with each wallpaper pattern
6 yards fine white lace edging, 1″ wide
⅛ yard crochet lace edging, 2½″ wide
Piece of ½″-thick Styrofoam, 11″ x 18″
Green powdered ''grass,'' one small bag
Spray adhesive
Small finishing nails
Wood glue
All-purpose glue
1 small white bead
Miniature artificial trees and shrubs
Two small hinges

The only "rent" you pay is the cost of the materials—and a little loving labor. The result, an intriguing new dollhouse, traditional Christmas-morning delight in any family with children. One of Gloria Vanderbilt's Victorian doll houses inspired the fashionable but compact version seen here. A modest 15¾″ wide by 10¼″ deep, it's made of ¼″ plywood, decoratively trimmed with strips of balsa wood. The front of the house swings open to reveal six well-furnished rooms. Shopping information for dollhouse wallpapers is on page 223.

You'll need a hand saw, coping saw, drill with ¼″ bit, an X-Acto knife, a small, flat paintbrush, medium to fine sandpaper and tweezers (optional) to complete this project.

Using dimensions indicated in Diagram 1, draw outline of front of house once and side of house twice on plywood. Mark outlines of windows and door. Using handsaw, cut out front and sides. To cut windows, make a hole in center of each window with drill, then use coping saw to cut openings as marked. Do not cut out door.

From plywood, cut one 15¼″ x 19½″ piece for back of house, one 9½″ x 15¼″ piece for base and one 9″ x 19¼″ piece for vertical partition inside house. Cut four pieces of plywood for floors, two 9″ x 9″ and two 6″ x 9″. Sand all surfaces and edges smooth, using medium and then fine sandpaper.

Paint one side of each piece for exterior walls of house yellow; allow paint to dry. Paint door area gray; allow to dry. Using X-Acto knife, cut strips of

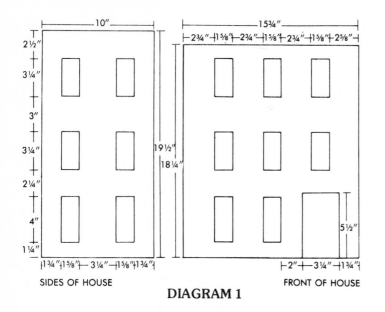

SIDES OF HOUSE   FRONT OF HOUSE

DIAGRAM 1

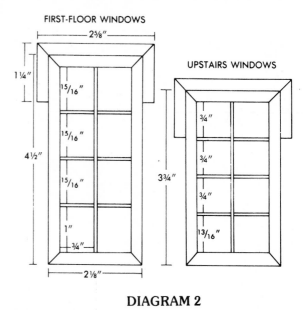

FIRST-FLOOR WINDOWS

UPSTAIRS WINDOWS

DIAGRAM 2

balsa wood to lengths indicated by Diagram 2 for trim around windows and for pane partitions; use $\frac{1}{16}"$ x $\frac{1}{4}"$ for pane partitions, $\frac{1}{8}"$ x $\frac{1}{4}"$ for outlining windows, and $\frac{1}{4}"$ x $\frac{1}{4}"$ for trim at top of windows, cutting ends of strips diagonally where indicated to make mitered corners. Paint the strips white, glue them together and then glue them in place inside and around window openings. (Using tweezers may make it easier to position strips accurately.)

Cut strips of balsa wood to lengths indicated by Diagram 3 for trimming on and around door: use $\frac{1}{16}"$ x $\frac{1}{4}"$ for paneling, $\frac{1}{8}"$ x $\frac{1}{4}"$ for outlining door, $\frac{1}{4}"$ x $\frac{1}{4}"$ for strip above door, $\frac{1}{8}"$ x $\frac{1}{2}"$ for strip above that, and $\frac{1}{4}"$ x $\frac{1}{4}"$ for top strip. Paint strips white and glue in place. Glue small white bead to door for doorknob.

Using Diagram 4 as actual-size pattern for trim along front edges of house, cut 34 pieces from $\frac{1}{16}"$ x $\frac{1}{2}"$ balsa wood; paint pieces white. When dry, glue 18 pieces in place at equal intervals down left edge of front, glue 16 pieces down right edge, leaving spaces for hinges after second piece from top and botton (see photograph).

Using Diagram 5 as actual-size pattern for supports under balcony, cut three pieces from $\frac{1}{4}"$ x $\frac{1}{2}"$ balsa wood. Diagram 6 shows center section and one side section of balcony. Cut a $12\frac{1}{4}"$-long strip of $\frac{1}{8}"$ x $\frac{1}{2}"$ balsa wood for floor of balcony. Following lengths indicated by diagram, cut $\frac{1}{16}"$ x $\frac{1}{8}"$ strips for horizontal and diagonal rails (for all three sections); cut four $\frac{1}{8}"$ x $\frac{1}{8}"$ pieces for posts. Glue pieces together as indicated by diagram and paint dark gray. When dry, glue to front of house with

floor of balcony $\frac{1}{2}"$ below third-story windows. Diagram 7 shows side view of balcony.

Glue and nail side walls to $19\frac{1}{2}"$ edges of back wall. Glue and nail back and side walls to three edges of base. Following spacing indicated by Diagram 8, glue edges of vertical partition inside house to back wall and base, then glue floors in place individually, gluing three edges of each one to side wall, back wall and partition.

From $\frac{1}{4}"$ x $\frac{1}{4}"$ balsa wood, cut one $19\frac{1}{4}"$-long strip, one $15\frac{1}{4}"$-long strip, two $9"$-long strips and two $6"$-long strips. Stain strips brown and glue to front edges of base, vertical partition and floors, covering raw edges of plywood. From $\frac{1}{8}"$ x $\frac{1}{4}"$ balsa wood, cut twenty $2"$-long strips for interior windowsills; stain brown and glue one along bottom edge of each window opening, centering it under window.

To complete interior, glue dollhouse wallpaper to back and side walls of each room, using a different pattern in each room; glue coordinating solid-color fabric or paper to floor of each room. To make curtains and valance for each window, cut three strips of $1"$-wide lace edging, two $3\frac{1}{2}"$ long and one $3"$ long. Glue short ends of $3\frac{1}{2}"$-long strips across top of window so long edges meet at center of window; glue one long edge of $3"$-long strip over them, across top of window, to form valance.

Diagram 9 shows actual-size side view of cornice around top of house. For front section of cornice, cut strips of balsa wood in sizes listed to following lengths, reading from bottom to top of diagram:

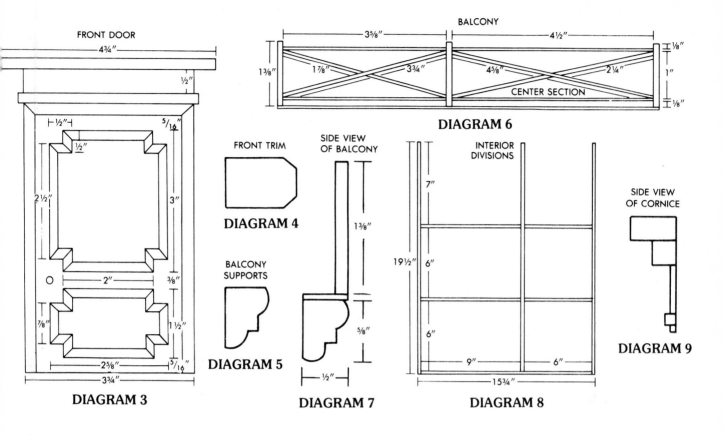

FRONT DOOR

DIAGRAM 3

FRONT TRIM

DIAGRAM 4

BALCONY SUPPORTS

DIAGRAM 5

BALCONY

CENTER SECTION

DIAGRAM 6

SIDE VIEW OF BALCONY

DIAGRAM 7

INTERIOR DIVISIONS

DIAGRAM 8

SIDE VIEW OF CORNICE

DIAGRAM 9

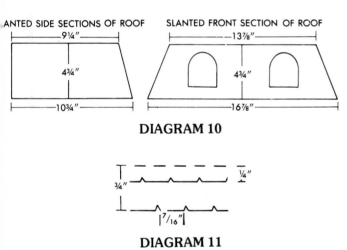

SLANTED SIDE SECTIONS OF ROOF

SLANTED FRONT SECTION OF ROOF

DIAGRAM 10

DIAGRAM 11

¹⁄₁₆″ x ¹⁄₁₆″, 15¾″ long; ⅛″ x ⅛″, 16″ long; ¹⁄₁₆″ x ½″, 15⅞″ long; ¼″ x ¼″, 16¼″ long; ¼″ x ½″, 16¾″ long. Glue strips together as shown in diagram. For each side section, omit bottom strip, then cut strips of the same sizes to following lengths: 10″, 9⅞″, 10¼″, 10¼″. Glue strips for each side section together, then glue side sections to top of house. Cut a strip of plywood 1½″ wide x 15¾″ long; glue front section of cornice to plywood strip, then place completed front section across front of house and glue to ends of side sections,

mitering corners. Cut two strips of ¹⁄₁₆″ x ½″ balsa wood, each 18¾″ long; glue one to back edge of each side of house, below cornice.

Using dimensions indicated by Diagram 10, cut one piece of plywood for slanted front section of roof, and two pieces for slanted side sections. Cut a 17″ x 10¾″ piece of plywood for base of roof, and a 9¼″ x 13⅞″ piece for top of roof. Glue and nail slanted front and sides to outer edges of base, mitering corners; glue and nail top to front and sides. (Base of roof forms ceiling for third story of house; space between base and top of roof can be left open in back and used for storage, or closed off by adding a piece of plywood to fit between slanted side sections of roof.)

For shingles, cut nine strips of ¹⁄₁₆″ x ¾″ balsa wood to same length as front section of roof; cut nine strips to same length as each side section. Using X-Acto knife, cut grooves in one edge of each strip as indicated by Diagram 11. Glue grooved strips in place on roof, overlapping ¼″ of each strip as indicated by diagram. Cut strips of ¹⁄₁₆″ x ¼″ balsa wood to fit across top edges of front and side roof sections, and down both sides of each front corner; glue in place over shingles.

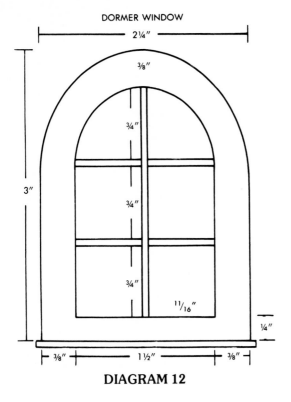

DORMER WINDOW

DIAGRAM 12

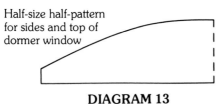

Half-size half-pattern
for sides and top of
dormer window

DIAGRAM 13

for sides and top of dormer windows; enlarge diagram to 3¾" long, complete pattern and cut two pieces from 1/16"-thick balsa wood. Wet each piece; curve to shape of dormer window (see Diagram 12). Glue curved edges to roof in positions indicated. Following Diagram 12, cut curved frames from 1/8"-thick balsa wood; cut pane partitions from 1/16" x 1/16" balsa wood. Cut 1/16" x 1/4" strip for base of each window. Glue frame, partitions and base for each window together; paint white. Cut and notch strips for shingles to fit across top and sides of each dormer; glue in place, overlapping as before. Cut a strip of 1/16" x 1/4" balsa wood to fit across center top of each dormer; glue in place in upright position. Cut two pieces of 2½"-wide crochet lace to shape of window frames and glue to inside edges for curtains. Glue edges of frames just inside front edges of dormers. Paint entire roof dark gray. When dry, mix lighter shade of gray paint and brush lightly over roof with vertical strokes to simulate uneven shading of real shingles.

Following lengths indicated by Diagram 14, cut strips of 1/16" x 1/8" balsa wood for roof railings; cut 1/8" x 1/8" strips for posts. (Only one-half of front railing is shown in diagram.) Glue railings and posts together and paint dark gray; glue in position around top of roof.

Hinge front of house to right side wall. With back edges flush, center house on Styrofoam; glue in place and nail through Styrofoam into walls of house. Spray edges and visible border of Styrofoam with adhesive; cover with powdered "grass." Add miniature trees and shrubs around house as desired.

For dormer windows, first cut away shingles from two areas where windows will be placed (see Diagram 10 and Diagram 12), and paint roof blue in those areas. Diagram 13 is half-size half-pattern

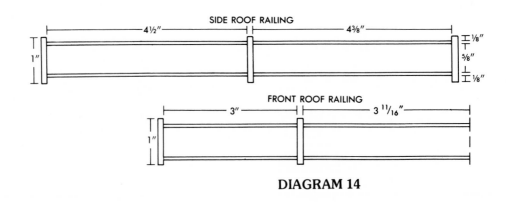

SIDE ROOF RAILING

FRONT ROOF RAILING

DIAGRAM 14

194

PIN-MONEY PRESENT: A NECKLACE MADE OF PAPER

That's right—this surprising necklace is made mostly of paper. The long, tapering beads are nothing but colorful triangles of paper cut from magazine pages and wrapped around wires. How's that for a fashionable present at a pittance? This happens to be one of Gloria's favorite necklaces, and you can copy it.

MATERIALS NEEDED

Colorful illustrations from slick-paper magazines
105 round beads, ¼" diameter
20 rectangular beads, ⅛" x ³⁄₁₆"
60 oval gold-colored jumprings, ¹⁄₁₆" x ³⁄₁₆"
Fine, stiff, gold-colored wire
½ yard gem monofilament (nylon necklace cord)
Necklace closure
Jewelry pliers
All-purpose glue

To make paper beads, cut 46 elongated triangles, each 2³⁄₁₆" wide at base and 5" long from center of base to point, from magazine illustrations. Cut a piece of wire 3¼" long. Beginning at base of one triangle, center and roll paper tightly around wire until close to pointed end; apply glue to pointed end and press in place, forming one bead. Cut additional pieces of wire and make 46 beads.

Thread wire at one end of each paper bead through 1 round bead; bend wire into a hook with pliers, add one jumpring and secure by closing hook tightly at top of round bead and inserting end of wire into bead hole.

To each of 20 beads, add a second jumpring: to do so, open second ring with pliers, slip one end into first jumpring and close second ring securely. At other end of each of the same 20 paper beads, bend wire into hook and add a second paper bead by slipping jumpring onto hook and closing hook securely. Attach remaining 6 beads to center 6 beads of second row in same manner. Thread a rectangular bead on each remaining wire; secure by bending wire into closed hook and inserting in bead hole.

To string necklace, thread one-half of necklace closure on one end of necklace cord; secure with a knot. String 20 round beads onto cord. Then alternate 19 round beads with jumprings of 7 double beads, then 6 triple beads, then 7 more double beads. Finish by stringing on 20 remaining round beads; attach other half of necklace closure and secure with knot.

GLORIA
IN
MINIATURE

THE SURPRISING TALE OF A REMARKABLE RAG DOLL

Once upon a time there was a glamorous doll named **Gloria.** Some people, totally lacking in imagination, called her a rag doll. But that was only because she was so easy to make—which, as you know, rag dolls usually are. But this doll was different from all other dolls. True, she was made of muslin and yarn and embroidery floss, but when she was all stitched together and delectably dressed in pink and white gingham checks and a ruffly organdy pinafore, something magical happened. She suddenly turned into a glamorous celebrity—a fashionable lady of great taste and talent who could do any number of artistic things, like painting and designing and decorating beautiful rooms. Now, wouldn't you like to have a doll like that? All the directions and diagrams you need to make this glorious doll and her pretty clothes follow.

"GLORIA" IS A WELL-DRESSED DOLL

Naturally, she's well-dressed. Like her fashionable look-alike, this remarkable rag doll is a lady of many talents—and one of them is always looking marvelous, whether she's wearing a glamorous long gown or casual work clothes. Make her party dress in a pretty cotton print, with an appliqué-trimmed panel of crisp white piqué. Make her overalls in patchwork-print cotton, the classic shirt in rugged blue denim. Or reverse the order and make the overalls in denim, the shirt in checked cotton.

"GLORIA" RAG DOLL

MATERIALS NEEDED

⅞ yard unbleached muslin
½ yard black iron-on tape, 1″ wide
⅓ pound polyester fiberfill
D.M.C six-strand embroidery floss; one strand each Pink, #776; Black, #310; Brown, #840
28 yards black four-ply knitting yarn
Embroidery hoop, 3½″ diameter (optional)
Dressmakers' tracing paper
Pink and brown indelible coloring pencils
Black sewing thread

Enlarge pattern on paper ruled in 1″ squares. Pin each pattern piece to fabric with arrow parallel to selvedge, following directions printed on pattern. Trace circles, X marks and dotted lines from pattern pieces onto fabric. ¼″ seam allowance is included on pattern pieces; cut along outside outline of each piece.

From muslin, cut one front section and one back section. From black iron-on tape, cut four shoe sections. Using dressmakers' tracing paper, trace facial features onto front section. Using three strands of floss in needle and following directional lines indicated on pattern, embroider pupils of eyes black and lips pink in satin stitch (Diagram 1). Embroider outlines of eyes black and shadow lines above outlines brown in backstitch (Diagram 2). Embroider brows and nostrils brown and lashes black in straight stitch (Diagram 3). Coloring lightly with coloring pencils, add a little pink to cheeks and light brown shadow above eyes. Press fabric on wrong side. Place shoe sections in position where indicated on front and back sections and press in place.

With right sides facing, stitch front and back sections together, leaving an opening on left side between marked circles. Clip seam allowances around curves and turn doll right side out. Stuff head, body and limbs with fiberfill; slipstitch opening closed.

Stitch across arms and tops of legs on dotted lines; center outside leg seams over inside leg seams and stitch across "knees."

To make rosettes on shoes, make six ⅜″ loops of black floss around circle on each instep, taking a backstitch between each loop to lock stitch in place (Diagram 4). Make a pink French knot in center of each loop, with two ⅜″ ends of floss forming part of rosette (Diagram 5).

Cut black knitting yarn into 15″ lengths. To attach yarn "hair," insert a single length of yarn in a sharp, large-eyed needle for each stitch; with doll facing you and working across top of head between circles on seam line, take ⅛″ stitches through fabric, removing needle after each stitch and pulling yarn until ends are even. Keep stitches very close together. Then attach another row of yarn hair across "hairline" on pattern. Smooth strands of yarn from temples down to side seams and pin in place at X marks on pattern. Draw yarn from top of head down to back of neck, poufing it slightly to add rounded height, and pin in place across back of neck. Using black sewing thread, backstitch strands firmly to sides of head at seam line and loosely across back of neck. Cut off ends of yarn in an even line 1″ below stitching and coax strands at sides of head to curve outward and upward.

DIAGRAM 1

Satin Stitch

DIAGRAM 2

Backstitch

DIAGRAM 3

Straight Stitch

DIAGRAM 4

Loops

DIAGRAM 5

French Knot

DRESS AND PINAFORE

MATERIALS NEEDED

1¼ yards pink-and-white checked fabric
⅞ yard white organdy, 44″ wide
⅞ yard white grosgrain ribbon, 1″ wide
¼ yard firm elastic, ¼″ wide
Dressmakers' tracing paper
2 snaps, 400

Enlarge pattern pieces on paper ruled in 1″ squares. Pin each pattern piece to fabric with arrow parallel to selvedge, following directions printed on pattern. Trace circles, X marks and dotted lines from pattern pieces onto fabric. ¼″ seam allowance is included on pattern pieces; cut along outside outline of each piece.

TO MAKE DRESS:

Only half-pattern for neckband is given; make full pattern for this piece before cutting fabric.

Cut two front sections and one back section, placing center line of back on fold. On front sections, turn ⅛″ of fabric to wrong side above circles and edge stitch. With right sides together, stitch front sections to back along overarm seams and across seam allowances. Clip to seam at neckline where indicated by dotted lines on pattern; press seam allowances open. Hem lower edges of sleeves with narrow double hems, taking up ¼″ allowance. Cut a 3½″-long piece of elastic and pin to inside of each sleeve, centering it over line indicated on pattern. Stitch in place, stretching elastic as you stitch to full width of sleeve. With right sides together, stitch underarm seam; press seam allowances open.

With right sides facing, stitch front sections together at center front, from lower edges to marked circle. Clip seam allowance of left front section on dotted line. On right front section, turn seam allowance to right side above circle and stitch across seam allowance at neckline to circle. Clip to circle on dotted line and turn seam allowance to wrong side. On left front section, clip on dotted line and turn seam allowance to wrong side; topstitch to circle. Press seam allowance on right front to wrong side; sew on snaps where indicated on pattern.

Fold neckband in half, right sides together; stitch ends and long edges together to circles. Clip seam allowances on dotted lines; trim allowances at points. Turn band right side out and press. With right sides together, stitch one side of band to neckline, matching circles at front; press seam allowances toward band. Turn seam allowance along other edge of neckband to wrong side and slip-stitch folded edge to neckline on wrong side, enclosing raw edge of fabric.

Turn ¼″ along bottom edge of dress to wrong side and edge-stitch. Turn up a ½″ hem and slip-stitch in place.

TO MAKE PINAFORE:

From organdy, cut two bib sections, two bib ruffles, one skirt section and one skirt ruffle, cutting skirt ruffle across entire width of fabric (pattern is for short section of ruffle only, to indicate width, hem allowances and gathering lines). From ribbon, cut one waistband.

Make two rows of gathering stitches across top of skirt and across upper edge of skirt ruffle, as indicated on patterns. Draw up gathering stitches on ruffle so ruffle fits lower edge of skirt. With right sides together, pin and stitch ruffle to skirt. Trim seam allowances to ⅛″ and press allowances toward skirt. Make narrow double hems along side and bottom edges, taking up ¼″ allowance. Draw up gathering stitches across top of skirt so edge of skirt fits between circles on lower edge of waistband. Place edge of ribbon over gathering stitches and topstitch between circles; press.

Bib of pinafore is made double; one bib section serves as lining. With right sides facing, stitch bib and lining together along inside edges of straps and across front. Clip seam allowances at corners and trim to ⅛″. Turn bib right side out and press. Turn side edges of both layers ¼″ to inside and press; trim to ⅛″. Make a narrow double hem along curved edge of each bib ruffle, taking up ¼″ allowance. Make two rows of gathering stitches along straight edge of each ruffle, as indicated on pattern. Draw up gathers so ruffle fits side edge of bib between circles. Trim seam allowances just beyond gathering. Pin gathered edge of each ruffle between bib and lining, with turned edges of bib covering gathering stitches. With right sides facing you, topstitch through all thicknesses.

PARTY DRESS

MATERIALS NEEDED

1 yard printed fabric, 48″ wide
⅝ yard white piqué, 44″ wide
2 yards white Venice lace edging, ½″ wide
¾ yard of elastic, ⅛″ wide
3 snaps, #00
Small scrap of fusible webbing
Dressmakers' tracing paper

Enlarge pattern pieces on paper ruled in 1″ squares. Broken lines indicate ¼″ seam allowances; arrows indicate lengthwise grain of fabric. Trace circles, X marks and dotted lines from pattern pieces onto fabric. Mark center fronts and backs within seam allowances.

From printed fabric, cut two back sections of dress; cut two belt sections, centering pattern over printed motif of fabric; cut one front section, placing center front line on fold of fabric. From white piqué, cut one neckband; cut one front panel, placing center line on fold. If white fabric is not opaque, cut two panels, baste together and handle as one. Stitch along side edges of panel, ¼″ from raw edges; clip curves and press seam allowances to wrong side just inside stitch lines. Cut two 22″ lengths of lace edging and baste to wrong sides of panel along turned edges, with decorative edges of lace extending ⅜″. Matching center fronts, neck and bottom edges, place panel on dress front. Fold each belt section in half lengthwise, right sides together, and stitch ¼″ from raw edges. With seam centered lengthwise, press along lines marked "fold." Stitch across slanted ends of belt, ¼″ from raw edges. Turn to right side. Place open end of belt between panel and dress at waistline, taking up ¼″ allowance. Pin panel to dress front. Edge-stitch along turned edges of panel through all thicknesses. Stitch panel to dress along neckline, ¼″ from raw edges; stitch the two together along bottom edges.

Cut three rose motifs from fabric and trim away background. Pin a piece of fusible webbing to back of each motif; trim to match outline of motif. Pin one motif to panel at left shoulder and two to right side of skirt, where indicated by X's on pattern. Press motifs in place.

On back sections of dress, turn ⅛″ of fabric to wrong side above circles and stitch. With right sides facing, stitch back sections together along center back seam line, from lower edge to circle. On left side, clip seam allowance along dotted line to circle. On right side, press seam allowance to wrong side along center back line. Press seam allowances open. With right sides facing, stitch front and back sections of dress together along overarm seam lines and across seam allowances at neckline. Clip and press seam allowances open. Stitch underarm seams and press allowances open.

At lower edge of each sleeve, turn ¼″ of fabric to wrong side. Turn up another ¼″ and edge-stitch along fold, leaving an opening at underarm seam for inserting elastic. Cut a 3½″ length of elastic for each sleeve. Using a pin, draw elastic through casings. Stitch elastic together ¼″ from ends.

Along one long edge of neckband, turn ¼″ of fabric to wrong side and press. Cut a 5¾″ length of lace edging; baste the straight edge along fold on wrong side of neckband and edge-stitch in place. With right sides facing, pin neckband to dress, matching center fronts and back edges; stitch together ¼″ from raw edges. Turn under ¼″ of fabric at right side edge of band; press. Turn under ⅛″ on left side and stitch. Sew on snaps where indicated by small X's. Turn ¼″ along bottom edge of dress to wrong side and edge-stitch. Turn up a ½″ hem and slipstitch in place.

OVERALLS AND SHIRT

MATERIALS NEEDED
⅝ yard printed fabric, 54" wide
¼ yard lightweight blue denim
¼ yard red fabric
2 gold nailheads, ⅜" diameter
5 snaps, #00
¼ yard elastic, ⅛" wide

TO MAKE OVERALLS:

Enlarge pattern pieces on paper ruled in 1" squares.

From printed fabric, cut two back sections, two front sections, two straps and one bib, placing center front line of bib on fold of fabric. From red fabric, cut three pockets.

Turn ¼" of fabric to wrong side all around each pocket and press; top-stitch across top ⅛" from folded edge. Pin one pocket to bib where indicated on pattern; stitch ⅛" from folded side and bottom edges. Note: all top stitching is done in red.

Turn side edges of bib to wrong side and press; top-stitch ⅛" from folded edges. Turn top edge ¼" to wrong side; top-stitch as before. With right sides facing, stitch front sections of overalls together at center front; clip seam allowances around curve and press open. Turn under ⅛" on left side above circle and stitch. With right sides facing and matching center fronts, stitch lower edge of bib to front of overalls. With right sides facing, stitch back sections together; clip allowances at curve and press open. Turn under ⅛" on left side above circle and stitch. Turn side edges above waist to wrong side and stitch as on bib. Turn top edge ¼" to wrong side and press. Pin pockets to back and top-stitch in place. With right sides facing, stitch front and back of overalls together along side edges, leaving left side open above circle; then stitch inner leg seam. Clip left side of back at circle; press seam allowances open.

Fold each strap in half lengthwise, right sides fac-ing; stitch along pointed end and long side ¼" from raw edges; turn right side out. Top-stitch ⅛" from all edges. With seamed edges of straps toward center, pin pointed end of each strap to top of bib, overlapping edge ¼". Pin other ends to top of back on wrong side of overalls; top-stitch ⅛" from edge through all thicknesses. Attach small nailheads to pointed ends of straps on right side; sew snaps on bib and straps where indicated by X's. At bottom edge of each leg, turn up ¼" of fabric, then turn up another ¼" and top-stitch. Sew snap to left side where indicated by X's.

TO MAKE SHIRT:

From blue denim, cut two front sections, one collar and one back section, placing center back lines on fold of fabric. Turn under front edges of shirt ⅛" and stitch. Press turned edges to wrong side on fold line. With right sides together, stitch overarm seams and across seam allowances at neckline. Clip allowances and press open. Stitch underarm seams, clip curves and press allowances open. Turn under ¼" at each sleeve edge; turn up an-other ¼" and stitch, leaving opening at seam for inserting elastic. Using a pin, draw 3½" length of elastic through each casing and stitch ends of elas-tic together.

With right sides facing, fold collar in half length-wise and stitch across ends. Trim points, turn to right side and press. With right sides together, pin underside of collar to shirt, matching front edges of collar to turned front edges of shirt; stitch. Press allowances toward collar. Turn ¼" on upper side of collar to inside and slipstitch to neckline, enclosing raw edge of fabric. Stitch ⅛" from edge across bot-tom edge of shirt. Top-stitch front edges and collar ⅛" from edge. Sew on snaps.

TO MAKE KERCHIEF:

From remaining red fabric, cut one triangle for ker-chief. Turn ¼" of fabric to wrong side along all edges; turn up another ¼" and edge-stitch. Trim excess fabric at ends of long bias edge.

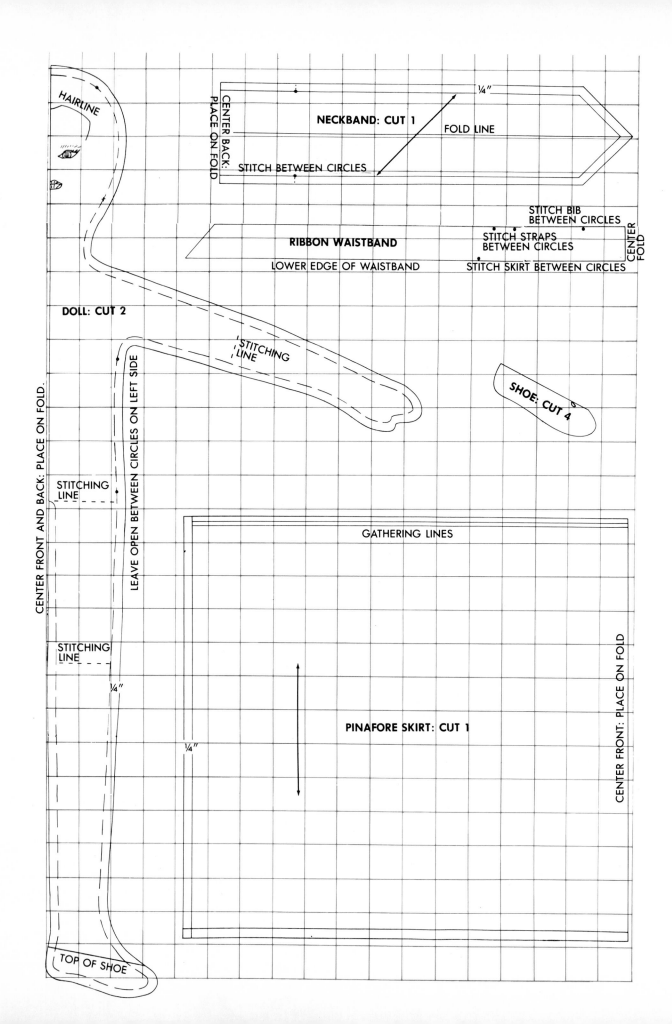

HAIRLINE

NECKBAND: CUT 1

CENTER BACK: PLACE ON FOLD

FOLD LINE

¼"

STITCH BETWEEN CIRCLES

STITCH BIB BETWEEN CIRCLES

STITCH STRAPS BETWEEN CIRCLES

RIBBON WAISTBAND

CENTER FOLD

LOWER EDGE OF WAISTBAND

STITCH SKIRT BETWEEN CIRCLES

DOLL: CUT 2

STITCHING LINE

SHOE: CUT 4

CENTER FRONT AND BACK: PLACE ON FOLD.

LEAVE OPEN BETWEEN CIRCLES ON LEFT SIDE

STITCHING LINE

GATHERING LINES

STITCHING LINE

¼"

¼"

PINAFORE SKIRT: CUT 1

CENTER FRONT: PLACE ON FOLD

TOP OF SHOE

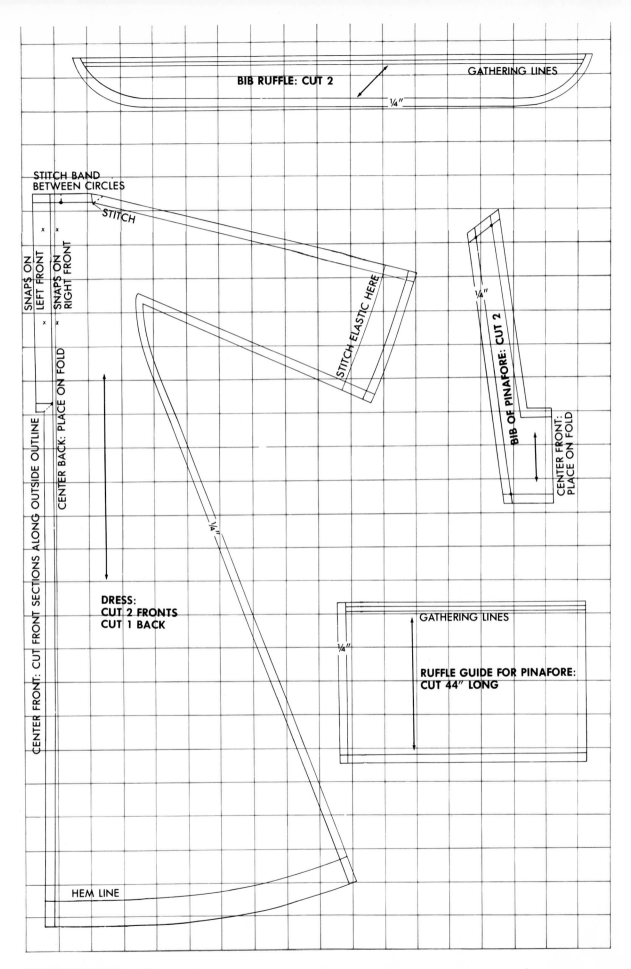

BIB RUFFLE: CUT 2

GATHERING LINES

¼"

STITCH BAND
BETWEEN CIRCLES

STITCH

SNAPS ON LEFT FRONT

SNAPS ON RIGHT FRONT

CENTER BACK: PLACE ON FOLD

STITCH ELASTIC HERE

¼"

BIB OF PINAFORE: CUT 2

CENTER FRONT: PLACE ON FOLD

CENTER FRONT: CUT FRONT SECTIONS ALONG OUTSIDE OUTLINE

¼"

DRESS:
CUT 2 FRONTS
CUT 1 BACK

GATHERING LINES

¼"

RUFFLE GUIDE FOR PINAFORE:
CUT 44" LONG

HEM LINE

EACH SQUARE = 1"

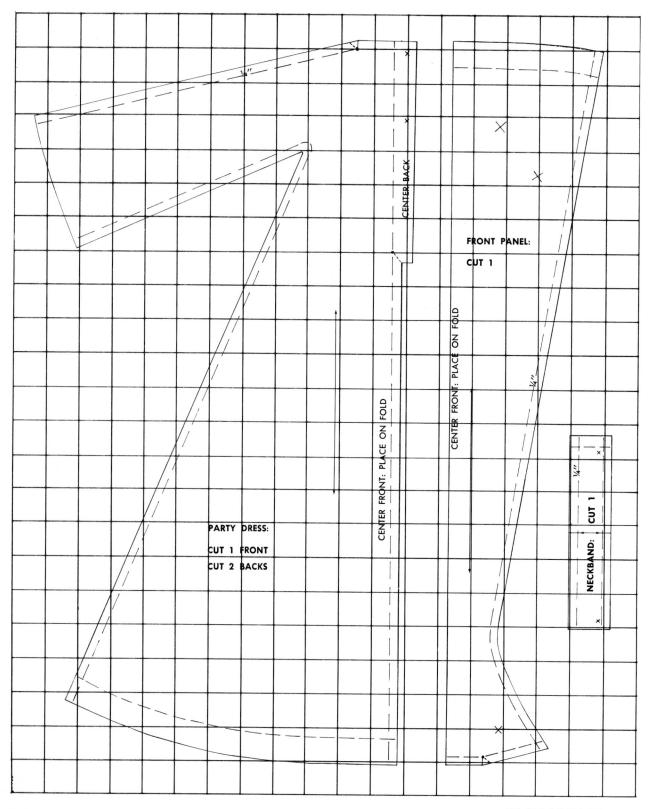

CENTER-BACK

FRONT PANEL:

CUT 1

CENTER FRONT: PLACE ON FOLD

CENTER FRONT: PLACE ON FOLD

¼"

PARTY DRESS:

CUT 1 FRONT

CUT 2 BACKS

¼"

NECKBAND: CUT 1

EACH SQUARE = 1"

208

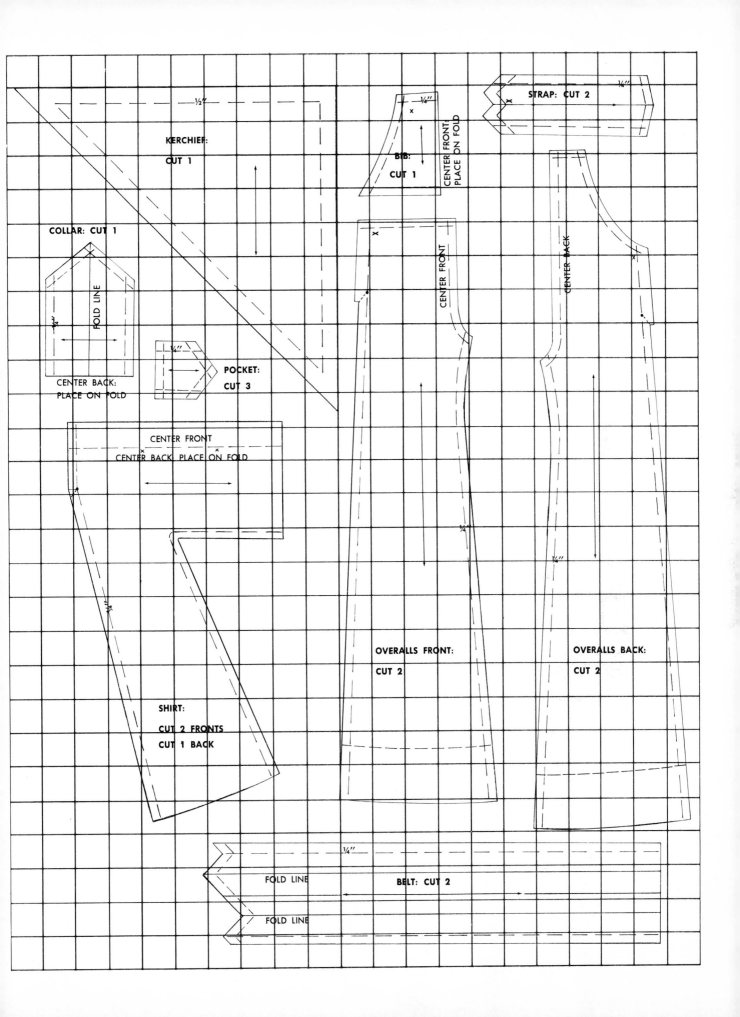

Loving
Greeting

May true
friends be
around you

COMPLIMENTS
OF THE SEASON.

MERRY CHRISTMAS

SHOPPING INFORMATION

Merchandise and materials listed can be ordered by mail. Prices may be subject to change. Please add sales tax where applicable.

DECOUPAGE AND CRAFT MATERIALS
from Adventures in Crafts, 218 E. 81st Street, New York, N. Y. 10028. Minimum order $9.00 plus $2.00 postage and handling.

PAGE 28:
Wooden hand-mirror base, 5″ wide, 12″ long, ¾″ thick; $3.50. Oval mirror, 3″ x 5″, to glue on front of wooden base, 75¢.

PAGE 29:
Wooden box with cut-out front and two separate panels for shadow-box effect, 9¼″ x 6¾″ x 4⅝″; $8.95. Victorian striped paper (also suitable for dollhouses), 17″ x 22″, $1.25 a sheet.

PAGE 30:
Roof-patterned dollhouse wallpaper, 8¾″ x 11½″, 35¢ a sheet.

PAGE 36:
Lacquered gilt papier-mâché tray, 12″ x 17″, $7.95.

PAGE 37:
"Redbird among Magnolias" decoupage print used on ginger jar, 6″ x 8″, 85¢.

PAGE 38:
Wooden "tooth fairy" box, 2½″ diameter, 1½″ high, $1.95.

Miniature wood treasure chest, 1⅞″ high, 2¾″ wide, 1¾″ deep; $1.75. Miniature metal hinges, 85¢ a pair.

Wooden pencil caddy, 4″ high, 3¼″ x 3¼″ square, $2.25.

Wooden cosmetic caddy, 2¼″ diameter, 2⅝″ high, $1.95.

PAGES 38–44:
Decorative "gold" paper braids: assortment of approximately 20 strips of embossed gilt paper borders from West Germany in seven different designs (including all those used in projects shown). #GB-PKG, $1.95

PAGE 39:
Italian gilt-framed, heart-shaped mirror, 5½″ high, 4⅝″ wide, ½″ deep, $4.95.

PAGE 42:
Round wooden "grandmother's gift" box, 4½″ diameter, 1¼″ deep, $4.95.

PAGE 43:
Small metal trays, 6¼″ x 8½″, undecorated, $1.75 each.

Adjustable wooden ring, 1⅝″ diameter, $1.00.

Wooden earrings with clip-on backs, 1″ diameter, $1.50 a pair.

Square wooden tissue-box cover, 5″ x 5″ x 5½″ high; $3.75. Heart-striped dollhouse wallpaper used to cover it, 11″ x 17″; 75¢ a sheet (two sheets required).

PAGE 44:
Miniature wood grandfather clock, 7″ high, 2″ wide, 1¾″ deep. Kit No. 690 includes clock movement and pendulum; $10.00.

Black metal letter holder, 4½″ high, 6″ wide, 3½″ deep, $2.50.

PAGE 171:
Metal matchbox cover for kitchen matches, 3″ x 5″; $1.95. Self-adhesive, velour-finish "Peel and Pat" in hot pink or blue, 9½″ x 12″, 98¢ a sheet.

PAGE 187:
End papers from Italy, in *fleur de lis* and griffin patterns, approximately 27½″ x 19½″; $1.75 a sheet.

PAGE 191:
Dollhouse wallpapers in assorted prints, 17″ x 22″; $1.25 a sheet. State predominant color desired.

WICKER SWAN AND BASKETS
from King's Ransom, 265 Danbury Road, Route 7, New Milford, Connecticut 06776.

PAGES 136–137:
Square wicker cache pot, approximately 9″ tall, $4.95 plus $1.00 postage and handling.

Large wicker swan planter, 21″ long, 23″ high; $29.95 plus $2.00 postage and handling.

PAGE 145:
Small wicker swan, 10″ long, 13½″ high; $9.95 plus $1.00 postage and handling.

SHELLS AND SHELL KITS
from Benjane Arts, 320 Hempstead Avenue, West Hempstead, New York 11552.

PAGE 142:
Everything needed to cover 24¼"-wide mirror with shells as shown: *Natica mamilla* shells in large, medium and small sizes, one tube of Bond 527 glue, plus 36-page catalog; $25.00 including postage.

36-page catalog separately, showing wide variety of shells available by mail, $2.00.

PAGE 145:
Everything needed to cover 10"-long wicker swan with shells as shown: two pounds of large pearled umbonium shells, ½ pound of medium-size Venetian pearl shells, one tube of Bond 527 glue, plus 36-page catalog; $25.00 including postage.

PAGE 155:
Voluta imperialis shell, approximately 5" to 6" tall; $10.00.

CONTRIBUTING DESIGNERS

JACK BODI
Pages 50–51: Vegetable designs for needlepoint pillows

SUSAN GOULD of THE FAMILY TREE
Pages 58–59: Tulip design for needlepoint triptych
Page 63: Adaptation of ''Pansies'' collage for needlepoint pillow
Pages 66–67: Needlepoint designs for ''Clarence'' and ''Claudette'' portraits
Page 71: Design for needlepoint bouquet
Page 75: Designs for needlepoint miniatures

TIELA PEARLMAN
Pages 147–149: Needlepoint designs for seashell ''paintings''